Ready to Preach II

Ready to Use Sermons and Worship Resources

Paul Gonzalez

WestBow
PRESS
A DIVISION OF THOMAS NELSON

WestBow Press books may be ordered through booksellers or by contacting:

WestBow Press
A Division of Thomas Nelson
1663 Liberty Drive
Bloomington, IN 47403
www.westbowpress.com
1-(866) 928-1240

Scripture taken from the King James Version of the Bible.

ISBN: 978-1-4497-8401-0 (sc)
ISBN: 978-1-4497-8402-7 (e)

Library of Congress Control Number: 2013902073

Printed in the United States of America

WestBow Press rev. date: 4/26/2013

Table of Contents

Worship Planning Helps #1

"Watch therefore, for ye know neither the day nor
the hour wherein the Son of man cometh."
- Matthew 25:13

WELCOME:

We extend a warm welcome to all who have come to worship together. May our time in God's presence prepare us to be ready and waiting for Jesus' return.

INVOCATION:

Most gracious God,

Prepare our hearts and minds to be ready for the soon return of Your Son, Jesus Christ. Empower us to lay aside all sin and to keep our lives burning brightly as a witness of Your mercy and love. Fill our hearts with joy and anticipation as we proclaim with confidence, "Come, Lord Jesus, come!" Amen

OFFERING PRAYER:

Dear glorious God,

You have blessed our nation, and we live in a land where You are worshipped, praised, and adored. Thank You for these tithes. Bless them for Your glory and bless us with Your fruits. In Jesus' name. Amen.

PRAYER FOR THE FAMILY OF GOD:

Dear Heavenly Father,

Thank You for this day to worship You. Thank You for Your precious Word that You have blessed us with, today. Bless everyone with it and bless our leaders and all those in authority. We lift up our President and those around him who are in positions of authority. We pray that their hearts may be humble before You. Give them discerning minds so they can make godly decisions. Give them courage and strength and faith as they face the challenges before them and our nation. May Your Spirit empower them and lead them in accordance with Your will. Give them vision and ability to rule in a way that peace and godliness may be in our land. Hear our prayer, O Lord, and bless our leaders in our country.

Bless those whom you have entrusted into our care. Give us and give them wise minds and humble spirits to do Your will and to know You more. We call upon Your power and glorious might to strengthen us with endurance and patience, joy, and gratitude until the day Jesus returns and gathers His church home. Amen.

BENEDICTION:

Brethren, just as you received Jesus Christ as Lord of lords, continue to worship Him and live for Him. May the Lord strengthen your faith and bless you with His Holy Spirit so you can have enough oil in your lamps for His coming. Amen.

SUGGESTED HYMNS:

"Shall We Gather at the River"
"When the Roll Is Called Up Yonder"
"When We All Get to Heaven"
"What a Friend"
"Mansion Over the Hilltop"
"Blessed Assurance"

Sermon #1:
"Is Your Lamp Burning?"

Matthew 25:1-13 & Revelation 8

Bible scholars and preachers have not stopped looking for future meaning from the parables. We, too, should always be looking forward to new information about the parables. One thing we know is that the Bible tells us, that in the last days, the earth is going to be filled with the knowledge of the Lord. We believe there is a treasure of nuggets lying in the parables preached by Jesus.

In today's parable, the ten virgins were invited to a wedding. Jesus proclaimed this parable to teach us the urgent need to always be prepared for Him. Is your lamp burning, church? We should have our names written in two books: the church directory and the Lamb's Book of Life. We must be prepared. Just having our names in the church directory does not mean the guarantee of Heaven. The truth of the matter is that the *Parable of the Ten Virgins* leads us to one important conclusion, found in the very last Scripture. In Matthew 25:13, Jesus tells us the very reason for this parable: "Watch therefore, for ye know neither the day nor the hour wherein the Son of man cometh." This is the answer to all of the questions people asked about this parable. But, if Jesus would have answered immediately, He would have destroyed the point of the message. So, let's keep it simple and wait for the conclusion.

In the *Story of the Ten Lepers*, nine were lost. In the *Parable of the Sower*, two thirds were lost. In the *Parable of the Talents*, one third was lost, and in the *Parable of the Ten Virgins*, one half was lost. They were lost; not because they were bad or evil people, not because they were unconcerned or mean, but because they were unprepared and lacked knowledge. They were ignorant of their calling and the warning to be ready.

That is what this parable is all about. It is about being ready to receive the Lord when He comes. It is about our spiritual fitness for entry into the festival chamber of the Bridegroom. It is about symbolism being what it is and understanding the skill of today's Bible scholars.

There was a professor in college who stated to his students, "When you are going to share about Heaven, let your expression light up with a smile. But, when you are going to share about hell, your every day face will do."

I want to go into three deeper points in this *Parable of the Ten Virgins*: the symbolisms, the lazy five virgins, and our readiness even at midnight.

First, let's look at the symbolisms. Jesus used many symbolisms in this parable. The main characters are the virgins. Numbers in the Bible have symbolism, and in this parable, there are ten virgins. Ten is the number of completeness. Jacob's wages were changed ten times which sets forth a complete disappointment outside the will of God and His Promised Land. Eliezer, the servant, took ten camels with him when he started from home in order to obtain a bride for Isaac. God gave His people Ten Commandments through Moses. Daniel and his three friends were proved ten days, and at the end of the test, they were ten times better than the others. Christ gave the *Parable of the Ten Pounds and Ten Talents*. Jesus healed ten lepers. The dragon of Daniel and Revelation had ten horns which represent ten kings. The tenth of the tithe belongs to God.

The ten virgins symbolize the church congregation; the ones who are prepared and the ones who are not prepared for the coming of the Lord. It was a traditional custom that people would choose ten female loved ones from the family to come in with the bridegroom. They all had to have a good reputation with the family. In this parable, the ten virgins are divided into two groups as soon as the bridegroom comes. The wise virgins with good works went in and got paid. The foolish virgins who made foolish decisions lost their pay and their chance to go in. James 1:22 says, "But be ye doers of the word, and not hearers only, deceiving your own selves." The ten virgins were all waiting for the Lord, but five of them were not receiving good spiritual nutrition. They were connecting with the wrong crowd and not faithfully attending worship services. To have faith without obedience is having a lamp without oil; and we need to refill our lamps with oil in church. In I Peter 1:5-9, Peter says, "Who are kept by the power of God through faith unto salvation ready to be revealed in the last time. Wherein ye greatly rejoice, though now for a season, if need be, ye are in heaviness through manifold temptations: That the trial of your faith, being much more precious than of gold that perisheth, though it be tried with fire, might be found unto praise and honour and glory at the appearing of Jesus Christ: Whom having not seen, ye love; in whom, though now ye see him not, yet believing, ye rejoice with joy unspeakable and full of glory: Receiving the end of your faith, even the salvation of your souls."

The lamp symbolizes our holiness and spiritual living while the oil symbolizes the Holy Spirit. The Apostle Paul tells us, in Romans 8:14, "For as many as are led by the Spirit of God, they are the sons of God." Church, is your lamp burning brightly or is it running low? "But seek ye first the kingdom of God, and his righteousness; and all these things shall be added unto you." (Matthew 6:33)

The foolish virgins did not realize their lack of oil until it was too late and the other virgins did not want to share the little bit they had left. In our spiritual lives, we must give every professed believer the benefit of any doubt, and in doing so, we must encourage others to be witnesses of their salvation to others which will serve to strengthen their own faith in Jesus

Christ. So, remember it is important to fellowship always with Christians. This way, we will not nap while we are waiting for our name to be called. It is not a chance to slip up or let our spiritual oil run low like the chimes on a clock waiting to sound. Church, are we ready?

Are we ready even at midnight? We like to envision Jesus coming on the clouds in full view with all of His glory. But, we could also be on the other side, coming with Jesus, seeing all the Christians with stretched out arms in full view. Have you ever thought how the end of the seven years of tribulation is going to be, on that last day, the last seven hours? We are going to hear a trumpet sound; and it is not going to be a sound of an instrument, but like the sound of a bomb or loud thunder. The enemy will think it is the opponent while we will think it is the enemy coming. But, the trumpet will sound better, not like other trumpets sound. This one day, after six hours have passed through the terrible tribulation, I Thessalonians 4:16 says, "For the Lord himself shall descend from heaven with a shout, with the voice of the archangel, and with the trump of God: and the dead in Christ shall rise first" and walk for one hour on the earth, and on the last hour, the seventh hour, after crying and hiding from the enemy and the dead, the light of God will shine and people who are in sin will think it is the sun shining out of the cloudy sky. But, the trumpet will sound loud, making every creature that is in sin kneel, facing down, covering its ears.

Meanwhile, the Christians are disappearing, and then, "we which are alive and remain shall be caught up together with the dead in the clouds, to meet the Lord in the air; and so shall we ever be with the Lord. Wherefore, comfort one another with these words." Praise God! Church, are you ready? Is your lamp burning?

The foolish virgins were too involved in material things. They put their trust in the things of the world. When they looked for the believers in Jesus, they were all gone, gone to be with the Lord in heaven. It was too late. Church, we are almost over the seven years of tribulation. Christ is coming soon! These foolish virgins, like so many today, think that there will be a time of wedding cry and the appearance of the bridegroom. When another trumpet sounds, there will be another earth quake and another big building breakdown. And do these people have time to confess Jesus as Lord of lords? It all happens in a blink of an eye. That's how much time one has to repent for their sins and sincerely ask Jesus into their heart. Dare you wait? Church, is your lamp burning?

Keep your lamps trimmed and burning with the confession of a saint waiting for the Lord Jesus Christ; not in any other name, but in Jesus the Messiah. If we don't worship in the name of Jesus Christ, we will be surprised, one day, to see our lamps go out, the hour we know not. Watch, therefore, and be careful who you fellowship with. Be quick and direct and move on. Some people look like Christians, act like Christians, sound like Christians, but their lamps have no oil. In the *Parable of the Ten Virgins*, they all appeared to be alike until the bridegroom came. So, let's be very careful because there will be no second chance. The five virgins could not buy oil at midnight, and they were not allowed back in the house. Sure, it was a lot of trouble for the virgins to dress up for the wedding feast, and have their lamps filled with oil and with them. But, the celebration was well worth it for the five virgins who had oil and went in with the bridegroom, and got their "pay day". Likewise, it takes a lot of effort and time to serve the Lord, today. But, when He comes, again, the eternal celebration of joy in heaven will be worth it all. So, let me close with this question: Is your lamp burning? Amen

Worship Planning Helps #2

"I am the vine, ye are the branches: He that abideth in me, and I in him, the same bringeth forth much fruit: for without me ye can do nothing."
— John 15:5

WELCOME:

We extend a warm welcome to all who have come to worship together. May we bow at Jesus' feet to be anointed and appointed to the work He has for us in His kingdom.

INVOCATION:

Heavenly, Father,

You have called us to be Your servants. Send Your Holy Spirit to enlighten our minds, purify our hearts, strengthen our wills, and lead us to live as faithful followers of Jesus all the days of our lives. Amen.

OFFERING PRAYER:

We bring unto You now, Lord, both our money and our lives to be used so others may be free. For Your kingdom and Your glory, bless and multiply these gifts in the name of Jesus, we pray. Amen.

PRAYER FOR THE FAMILY OF GOD:

Jesus,

You are the Master of speaking the truth in love. You are both our Gentle Shepherd and Strong Deliverer. We desperately need Your love and Your truth. People all around us desperately need Your love and Your truth. Speak to and touch those who are hurting and afflicted, lost and lonely. Bring Your healing presence into their hearts and lives. Lift them up and secure them safe in You. All Your labor is done in love. May it be clearly evident that we are Your followers as we minister in love to one another and to our neighbors. Lord, I pray for each and everyone here. Lord, bless them dearly and meet their special needs. May Your love be with them and their families. Multiply Your love in and through us, Your servants, in Jesus' name. Amen.

BENEDICTION:

In the name of Jesus, go out and present yourself to others as one appointed and anointed, a worker who does not need to be ashamed and who correctly handles the Word of truth. God bless you and protect you this coming week. Amen.

SUGGESTED HYMNS:
"Heavenly Sunlight"
"In the Service of the King"
"Close to Thee"
"Make Me a Servant"
"Where He Leads me"

Sermon #2:
"Anointed and Appointed"

Exodus 3:1-20 & Psalm 90

Are there right and wrong reasons for working in the church? In this time of small congregations, most pastors are willing to accept any offers for service from the members of their church. But, they need to make sure that they are going to be at their job every time there is church. You can be appointed and anointed for a church job. We just need to be fair with God and with the church and we will receive spiritual strength through His Spirit.

We don't need for this work to be disruptive for us. If we mean business with God, let's give Him our very best and for the right reasons. We don't have to feel a need to make up for the past wrongs. Christians who have not yet grasped the full meaning of grace still feel the need to make up for their pasts. But, we know that no one can atone for their own sin. Only Jesus can do that. He paid it all on the cross at Calvary.

Some people serve because of tradition and their family who has always been a part of the church. "Grandfather was an usher, so now it is my turn to be an usher." If you are called into the position that belonged to grandfather, this is a service that is handed down from God to grandfather to you. Serve faithfully!

Some people serve God to win His approval and acceptance. But, we serve God out of our love towards Him. God cannot approve of us any more than He already has. God accepts us completely. If we enter into His service to receive His approval or anyone else's approval, we continue in bondage to the works of the Scripture that Paul states in Ephesians 2:8. "For by grace are ye saved through faith; and that not of yourselves: it is the gift of God." For if work gains God's approval, then, what would happen when a faithful worker gets sick and no longer serves? Do they lose God's approval? You know that service based on approval is a no win situation.

Service under any circumstance may result in personal satisfaction and gratitude from others and benefit those whom we serve. But, in some instances, it can result in more problems if the reason for serving is wrong to begin with. But the right reason for service comes from a true heart of faith, granting us freedom to serve Jesus by serving others. The person who serves with success will receive God's credit. They will not be puffed up or have pride to the extent that they enjoy the applause of a job well done; unless it pleases God and the reason for service comes out of a sense of gratitude that creates in them a sense of obligation. And that obligation, my brethren, is to love our neighbor as ourselves. In Galatians 5:13 and 14, Paul preaches to the Galatians: "For, brethren, ye have been called unto liberty; only use not liberty for an occasion to the flesh, but by love serve one another." For all the law is fulfilled in just one word, 'Thou shalt love thy neighbor as thyself.'" (Matthew 22:39)

It is ironic that those who have the right motivation are often afraid to serve for fear that they will somehow fail God. The same thing happened with Moses, the son of Pharaoh's daughter, who had been transformed through forty years of living out in the desert. He became an Arabian shepherd herding the flock of Jethro on Mount Horeb. Then, the scriptures say that he became the son-in-law of Jethro. Moses had to give up his wealth and fame in Egypt in exchange for humility and his position for his Hebrew people. What would people say about his life? Nothing! Shepherding sheep in the desert was much different than sitting on the throne in Egypt. But, it was here in the wilderness that God spoke to him saying, "Moses, Moses." So, it is through our lonely times that God speaks to us, too. But, Satan interrupts our messages by feeding us lies at work and in other places. But, we need to keep our eyes focused on God's promises. Moses was called to Mount Horeb to receive his divine instruction; just as we are called to receive God's divine promises through reading His Word. God speaks to Moses from a burning bush, expressing His sorrow at the oppression of Israel. God speaks to us from the church pulpit expressing His sorrow at the oppression of His people. Then, God sends Moses into Egypt saying, "I will send thee and I will be with thee." It must have sounded like a soft loving voice to the shepherd who had failed before.

I can relate to that. When I was seventeen years old, I started reading the Bible. But, I continued to pray to God and to Mary. You know, I came out of the Catholic doctrine and I was taught to pray to idols like Mary. Then, one evening, God told me not to bow down before idols. I didn't think Mary was an idol until God told me she was. The last time God told me to stop worshipping Mary was when he told me, "I will disintegrate your body and bring your spirit before my judgment and I will put away your soul in my warehouse." It was then that I decided to follow Jesus and only Him.

With one command, Moses is drafted to the stormy front line as God's messenger for freedom. Moses responds, "Who am I, that I should go unto Pharaoh, and that I should bring forth the children of Israel out of Egypt?" (Exodus 3:11) This sounds as though Moses is expressing unmanliness. But actually, it is not that, it is lowliness. His former confidence had all been beaten out of him. But, there was a time when he was ready to deliver the Hebrews with his own hand. But, those days were gone and age and loneliness and communion with God had mellowed him into humility. His beginning was as if he was shrinking; like some feel when they are called for the task. You don't have to be a prophet or a religious leader to have that same feeling. Those who accomplish their work, seldom start with confidence and self-assurance. Self confidence is not the strength that God uses for His instruments. He prefers to work with bruised reeds and He prefers to breathe His own strength into them. It is only when people say, "I can't do it." that they are fit for God to use.

Moses knew enough of Egypt that he stands before Pharaoh and he has no choice but to obey God. Moses prays for help and God answers him swiftly. God deals gently with our weakness. He immediately tells Moses, "Yes, I will be with thee." Moses' determination opens the door to God's help. God cannot help those who feel they can do it alone. If Moses had been self-confident, he would have no longing for God and no promises of God's presence. In all of our tasks in church work, we have the same assurance. Whenever we feel the task is too great for us, it is then that the strength of God's promises is ours. Hebrew 13:5 tells us "for he hath said, I will never leave thee, nor forsake thee."

God never appoints someone for service without anointing them with the skills to accomplish the job. Moses figured the difference between him and the strength of Pharaoh's kingdom. But, he left one thing out of the formula and that was God. God and His chosen messenger are always stronger than the adversary. It was needless for God to discuss with Moses his ability to manage the king of Egypt. The question was: Was God able to do it? Yes, "with God all things are possible." (Matthew 19:26)

God is patient with us just as He was with Moses. Remember our disappointment is God's appointment with us. He will allow us to question His appointment until, after a process of stripping us, we come to the point in our faith where we "...take pleasure in infirmities, in reproaches, in necessities, in persecutions, in distresses for Christ's sake: for when I am weak, then am I strong." (II Corinthians 12:9 & 10) For no human could reign victoriously over the hardened heart of Pharaoh. No human can build the kingdom of God on this earth. For we serve a mighty God who is able to use us to accomplish His will. He fills us and makes us into a vessel of His design. There is an adjustment in our goal and purposes which transforms us into the likeness of God's image. And when the transformation is completed, God's anointing runs all over us to do His will! For whom God anoints, He appoints! And we are His anointed and appointed ones.

Psalm 133 says, "Behold, how good and how pleasant it is for brethren to dwell together in unity! It is like the precious ointment upon the head, that ran down upon the beard, even Aaron's beard: that went down to the skirts of his garments; As the dew of Hermon, and as the dew that descended upon the mountains of Zion: for there the Lord commanded the blessing, even life for evermore." Amen!

Worship Planning Helps #3

"With men this is impossible; but with God all things are possible."
– Matthew 19:26

WELCOME:
We extend a warm welcome to all who have come to worship together. May we draw near to God and find strength, peace, and joy to face the trials and temptations of life.

INVOCATION:
Here we are, Lord, in Your presence. Quiet our restless thoughts and capture our wandering hearts that we might truly worship You. Help us to seek You above everything else and to worship You in the beauty of Your holiness and the faithfulness of Your love. In Jesus' name, Amen.

OFFERING PRAYER:
Father,
You have graciously given us Your Spirit of wisdom and Your Spirit of adoption. As Your grateful children we offer ourselves back to You with these gifts. Bless them and us for service in Your redeeming work. Amen.

PRAYER FOR THE FAMILY OF GOD:
Dear Heavenly Father,
In the name of Jesus Christ, God of the future, we need Your Spirit to lead us forward into a new day we have yet to understand fully. Teach us what we need to know in every moment so our lives may take the shape of our Lord with every decision we make. Bring to our attention those situations where we may contribute to growth and healing. Whether they are at home, at church, at school, or in the work place, we ask that You increase our understanding so we may act on Your behalf. Equip us to respond to the needs we see. Empower us to work with You so all may know the hope that Your Spirit brings.

I ask You to bless my brothers and sisters in the Lord. Show them a new revelation of Your Word with power. With Your Holy Spirit, I ask You to minister to our spirits. Where there is sin clogging the way, wash it down and clear the pathway. Break its hold over our loved one's life. Where there is pain, give us Your healing. Where there is self-doubting, renew our confidence in Your ability to work through them. In our tiredness and exhaustion, I ask You to bless us with strength and air to breathe the breath of God that we may be able to lead as Your servants. I ask You to renew us by revealing Your presence as Your Holy Spirit draws us into a closer relationship with You, O Lord. Bless us with a gift of discernment to reveal the evil forces around us and to use Your power to defeat them through prayer in Jesus' name. Amen.

BENEDICTION:

God has given you the Holy Spirit to transform you into the children of God you were created to be. Go and share with others that they may know they are God's children and our brothers and sisters, as well. Amen.

SUGGESTED HYMNS:

"We Have Come Into This House"
"As the Deer"
"In the Garden"
"In the Presence of Jehovah"
"Leaning on the Everlasting Arms"
"Turn Your Eyes Upon Jesus"

Sermon #3:
"God Can Change Things"

Exodus 33:12-23; John 1:6-18; Psalm 91

Have you ever been in a situation where you didn't feel God's Spirit or felt that your bond with God had been broken? Maybe, you are going through a spiritual or physical trial that is so great you feel as if God just turned away from you. Or maybe, you just neglected your relationship with Him and you find yourself in a place you never wanted to be; and now, your worshipping faith has stopped focusing on how God can change things in life. Have you slowed down on your praying or have you stopped caring about God? Well, let's be very careful because one moment's separation will hit hard like a ton of bricks. It all starts by skipping church. But, whatever the reason, separation from God will be a painful experience.

For the Israelites, it was their disobedience, the golden calf, that broke their bond; and now, idolatry. They had not been out of Egypt for more than a short while when the old habits and traditions of idol worship started in the camp or church. But the worst part was that even the leadership stopped going to church. Aaron sought to calm their desires by shaping a golden calf from all the wealth they had taken with them. Shaped by his own hands as a black smith, the Bible says he fashioned it together with a graving tool and built an altar for it. Where was Moses through all of this? He is on top of the mountain, talking to Yahweh. What a difference in leadership! One is praying to Yahweh while the other ones are turning their backs on Yahweh.

Then, Moses comes down from Mount Sinai, full of the Spirit of God, and returns to camp to find sin. He asked Aaron, "Why? Why did you lead the people away from Jehovah?" Aaron replied, "Moses, the people made me do it! All I said to them was throw your gold rings and bracelets, necklaces and earrings into the fire. And then, we all made this golden calf." Aaron thought like most people do when they get caught up in sin; he blamed others. Aaron thought he was doing great, but great is never measured in terms of what we do, but in what we are.

The Lord says, "I have called you and placed my potential for greatness on the inside of you." Let me ask you: Are you of God? Is God with you? Nicodemus said to Jesus, "Rabbi, we know that thou art a teacher come from God: for no man can do these miracles that thou doest, except God be with him." (John 3:2) Is God with you? Then, let's try to be more like Jesus!

So, separation from God is bad, but blaming others for your separation is like rubbing salt in an open wound. Aaron was flirting with sin and it developed into the sin of omission; not doing those things he was supposed to do. Then, that sin developed into the sin of commission; doing things he was not supposed to do. James 2:10 says, "For whosoever shall keep the whole law, and yet offend in one point, he is guilty of all." Some people say, "I would have never gotten into this mess if God would not have chosen me. I would have never gotten caught if He would have minded His own business. I would have never lied if the truth had remained hidden." It is better to declare the truth and be rejected than to withhold it just to be accepted.

Have you ever heard this before: God can change things? The story of Israel's worship of the golden calf is a good example of what happens when we sin and let our bad conscience be our guide. The Israelites were letting their bad conscience, which occupied their minds, rule over their body, soul, and spirit. We're all familiar with these trials. There is not a day that goes by that our mind does not battle against our body, soul, and spirit. The old conscience says, "They don't like me, and I don't like them, either." But the law of the Spirit says, "Love your enemies, bless them that curse you, do good to them that hate you, and pray for them which despitefully use you, and persecute you." (Matthew 5:44) Our old conscience says, "I'm tired of being around people who just won't do good." But the new conscience says, "We then that are strong ought to bear the infirmities of the weak, and not to please ourselves." (Romans 15:1) The old conscience says, "She thinks she is better than everybody else." But, the law of the Spirit says, "Let us therefore follow after the things which make for peace, and things wherewith one may edify another." (Ephesians 4:12)

It is a real challenge, trying to keep the mind clear. That is why Christians commit offenses, and feel miserable about it, while sinners feel no remorse at all. That is because we are in confession, at all times, and have a clear conscience. A clear conscience is one of the best friends we can ever have. It is like a compass guiding our hearts to God.

The Israelites were suffering because of lack of knowledge and of faith; not knowing the solution which was to cause a change to take place in their hearts, a resurrected spirit. But, Moses knew that he could not do it alone, not without God. So, he melted down the golden calf and ground it into a powder and sprinkled it into the Israelites' water supply. Then, he left the camp to pray to God. Moses left the camp and took the tabernacle with him, because God was no longer with Israel. And just to let you know where this tabernacle is now, it is in God's room in Heaven. Israel's sin had caused Moses to pick up the tabernacle and leave.

Let me ask you, this morning: How far do you have to go to get away from sin? In Hebrews 12:1, Paul says, "Wherefore seeing we also are compassed about with so great a cloud of witnesses, let us lay aside every weight, and the sin which doth so easily beset us, and let us run with patience the race that is set before us." Moses had to pray for answers to some tough questions. But, how was he going to get Israel to the Promised Land, now, if they would not behave and go to church? Israel had just seen Moses' anger as he broke the stone tablets God had just blessed them with. They were in sin as Moses destroyed the golden calf, and then, left taking with him the Lord's tabernacle. They all stood by their tents looking at Moses taking away from them the tabernacle. Now, they waited in silence for their indictment from Yahweh. Israel was worried about how they were going to get to the Promised Land. They knew they would eventually get there; but, who was going to lead them? Now, they faced the consequences of their disobedience. What penalties would they have to suffer along the way to the Promised Land?

Moses went off to pray. The common expression among Christians is prayer. We always pray for people who find themselves in difficult situations. God can change things, and for Moses, there were three important parts to keep these people together. First, Moses had to pray for these people. Now, before an intercessor can pray for others, he has to be sure his own body, spirit, and soul are right before God. Moses talks to God and says, "Show me the way that I may know Thee." Moses wanted to be prepared for any situation with Israel. Moses wanted a deeper knowledge, wisdom, and understanding of God. He wanted God's favor. He longed for a better fellowship, a better connection. "When shall I come and appear before God?" (Psalm 42:2) Prayer reveals the mind of God, and causes the sunshine of Jesus Christ to shine through us. There is nothing wrong because we look for the grace of Jesus. We are here in church, seeking His favor, wanting to understand the depth of His purpose and His plan. The only way we can lead is to ask God for help to bear the weight of the task. How could Moses lead unless he was first equipped? How can a farmer sow without seed? How can a Christian defend himself without the Word of God? God smiles His approval on His servants. He smiles when we trust Him and obey Him when He calls us to come to church.

Secondly, Moses trusted God. Moses asked God to extend His kindness to Israel. He identifies himself with them as partakers of God's mercy. He asks God to forgive their sins, and to please return to the camp to dwell with Israel. If God would be with them, it would be clearly visible to the wandering tribes that God was upon Israel. Have you prayed for your neighbor, lately? "Bless me and bless my neighbor, too. Bless me and bless my family, too." These are prayers of intercession. They are effective if they come from a contrite heart seeking God. God was pleased with Moses. Moses is a foreshadow of the role of Jesus Christ in the future. He knits himself so closely with us, just as Moses did with Israel. Jesus brings us continually before God. Moses trusted God completely because his prayer prevailed; just like Jesus, God delights in us because of His Son. The self-sacrificing love of God is a live picture of the cross in God's den; the cross of Calvary. The Bible declares that Jesus reigns in Heaven and sits on the throne at the right hand of God, and He lives to make intercession for us. (Hebrews 7:25) God delights in you!

Now, my third and final point: God grants Moses' requests. Moses' spirit is soaring on the wings of gratefulness. What servant worthy of God's delight would not want to abide in God's presence? Study the Bible, and what follows next, is the icing on a cake. Moses reveals himself strong in the Lord, and now, he wants to appear in the glory of God. Moses says to God, "I beseech thee, shew me thy glory." This is the cry of a heart with the astounding conscious of God's favor and the joy of answered prayer. God can change things. Moses is so strong in the Lord that his soul cries out for the impossible. Now, he wants to see God! God never refuses a broken and a contrite heart, but He may not give us everything we desire in the way we want it, but in God's way, all things are "Yes and Amen!" Moses asked to see God's glory and He saw God's goodness. He asked to see God's face, and he saw God's backside; because that is all flesh can handle and it is all you and I can handle. But one day, we will see Him in the natural, because "we are confident, I say, and willing rather to be absent from the body, and to be present with the Lord." (II Corinthians 5:8) When we pray and trust God, He will grant our requests, because we abide with Jesus and we are committed to Him. If Moses could pray, in the name of the Lord Jehovah and Yahweh, and be blessed, how much more can we be blessed who know the name of Jesus? "[For] at the name of Jesus every knee should bow, of things in heaven, and things in earth, and things under the earth; And that every tongue should confess that Jesus Christ is Lord;" the One who sits on the throne to make intercession for us. And this is why God can change things! Amen.

Worship Planning Helps #4

"My brethren, count it all joy when ye fall into divers temptations."
– James 1:2

WELCOME:

We extend a warm welcome to all who have come to worship together. May we rest in His unfailing power and love to bring us safely through the trials and temptations of life.

INVOCATION:

Our Father, who art in Heaven, Hallowed be Thy name. Thy kingdom come, Thy will be done, on earth as it is in Heaven. Give us this day, our daily bread, and forgive us our debts as we forgive our debtors. And lead us not into temptation, but deliver us from evil. For Thine is the kingdom and the power and the glory forever. Amen.

OFFERING PRAYER:

We bring unto Thee our tithes and offerings, knowing that they are acceptable unto Thee only to the degree that we have lived out justice and righteousness. May this offering be a sign of our love for You and a sign of our agreement with Your ministry of justice. In Jesus' name, Amen.

PRAYER FOR THE FAMILY OF GOD:

In the name of Jesus Christ, God of justice and God of mercy, we worship and praise Thee. For You are a God of joy; and You desire a life filled with joy for us. Through fear or pride, we often deny ourselves and others this joy which You desire for us. And yet, You come to us, seeking to bring sanity and serenity. In a time when people face one another in a hurry to gain more, You stop to bless us and heal the hurting. Your mercy is evident to us in all the wonders of creation, in the gathering of the church, in the awesome gift of faith, and of Your love in Jesus Christ for us. Even as we worship Thee as being our justice and mercy, we are aware that this world has not yet come into the fullness of Your reign. There are some who are oppressed by systems and addictions. There are many who are hungry, ill, homeless, and poor. Pain and disease and death are all around. Help us to be moved to do justice and mercy with Your Spirit's help. Teach us, O Lord, to reach out to one another for only then will we be able to perceive the power we have, as a community, to deal with life in a way that will bring joy and not sorrow. Touch our brethren who are facing trials, temptations, and tribulations. Strengthen them with Your everlasting fruits. Transform our lives that we may proclaim our faith with joy through all our circumstances.

Bless those who are sick, today, Lord. I pray for strength and healing for them through Jesus' name. I, also, pray for all who are here, today. Bless them and heal them and answer the cries of their hearts with Your special touch. In Jesus' name, I pray for Your kingdom to come and Thy will to be done on earth as it is in heaven. Amen.

BENEDICTION:

Go ye into all the world and seek justice. There, you will find the Lord at work already. Join Him and receive Your blessing to bless others. Amen.

SUGGESTED HYMNS:

"This Is the Day"
"He Leadeth Me"
"Sweet Hour of Prayer"
"In the Presence of Jehovah"
"Leaning on the Everlasting Arms"
"Blessed Assurance"

Sermon #4:
"Being Justified Through Trials and Temptations"

Psalm 103:1-8, Luke 8:4-15, James 1:1-8

James is a good book on how to overcome trials and temptations as well as how to find strength to continue as Jesus will carry your weight upon His shoulders. You know, our lives are filled with unexpected valleys of trouble from the start to finish. One of life's most difficult things is that trials and temptations will always come our way, no matter what. These trials and temptations are allowed by God to mature us spiritually. Nobody likes trials, but everybody likes the results they bring. They prove our love for God; and overcoming temptations will serve as a discipline to purify our faith. Patience means to continue with the opportunity to overcome in joy; not laying down and playing dead in difficult circumstances. We are in a training program for eternity, and God is giving us opportunities to grow, and use our faith to gain the victory in Jesus.

Trouble is something that will torture the innocent and the guilty. It does not matter what race we are, our age, educated or not, rich or poor, religious or non-religious, small or great, sinner or saint, we will all have trouble. The book of James says, "My brethren, count it all joy when ye fall into divers temptations." I wonder what James was thinking about when he said, "My brethren, count it all joy when ye fall into divers temptations." I don't know about you, but I count my troubles and problems a bother, my trials and temptations an irritation. I count my aches and pain a frustration. I don't really need to tell you how bad temptation and trials can get, because we all go through them. When trouble comes, it will make a success feel like a failure. It will make a blessing feel like a burden. It will make a joyful heart feel like a broken heart. It will make a mountain feel like it is higher. It will make a valley feel wider. It will make our backslides seem endless. When troubles attack our lives, our paradise turns into a prison. It turns a firm, solid foundation into quick sand. Trouble will make those that have hope seem hopeless. It causes the most peaceful person to become confused. It shakes you when you want to keep on. Brother James says that trouble can do all of these things. As ministers, we even have to preach to ourselves, when we are going through troubled times; and we have to count it all joy! Brethren, we must admit that his is a strange philosophy. Let's take a look at James 1:1-8 and see how and why James wants us to count it all joy.

One of the greatest blessings of Christianity is its power to unite us when we are in a group and in one spirit and one mind. In Philippians 2:2, Paul says, "Fulfill ye my joy, that ye be likeminded, having the same love, being of one accord, of one mind." Once we become Christians, we are bound together with grace. We are able to call ourselves brothers and sisters in the Lord; members of the same family of God, redeemed by the blood of the lamb, connected by the Spirit of God. Brother James shows a true brotherly kindness with believers in the midst of their trials. James went through these trials with his brethren. Like James, I declare that we have a higher calling, a duty to elevate and encourage our brothers and sisters who are in trouble and despair. Do not join the enemy!

James does not say, "If you fall or you might fall, but when you fall into different trials and temptations." It is not a matter of IF we will have trials and temptations in our lives. It is a matter of WHEN they come. All of us are in one of three positions: we are facing a trial, in the midst of a trial, or coming out of a trial. This is why we need to be understanding and encouraging when others are facing their trials and temptations. This is why we need to be in church; to know how to deal with life. We have a responsibility to help bear one another's burdens, not to destroy one another. I may not be you, today or right now, but all it takes is time. James says, "When you fall." The word 'fall' here means that trials and temptations will come unexpectedly and will catch you off guard, too. They are unpredictable and unplanned; when we least expect them. Sometimes, when we think we are over it. BAM!!! Another problem arises. James says, "When you fall into divers temptations." This means many temptations.

Some folks want a life with no hardships, no problems, no sorrows, no disappointments, no frustrations, no burdens, no cares, no suffering, no sickness, and no troubles. They just want to walk through life. But, I am amazed at the things God sends His children through. You would think that if God is going to select a person or people to work for Him, He would safeguard them from all trials and temptations. It seems strange that He would call me and then, send me through trials and temptations. We need to know and accept the fact that there will be times and season in our lives when it seems like everything that can go wrong will go wrong. We need to know how to handle ourselves when things go from bad to worse. It is then, that a person's relationship with God is tested. How will we respond? Will that mole hill become a mountain when everything in life either falls apart or seems to go wrong? What do you do when the shallow ditch becomes a deep valley and the shallow stream becomes a raging sea? What do you do when a gentle cub becomes a roaring lion and the harmless lizard becomes a fire dragon or when you are crossing dangerous rivers and the bridge breaks? What do we do when the trials and temptations come and we are not ready for them?

So, when we face difficulties, we either respond in joy unto the Lord or we react negatively and lose our steadiness. Our response will be the indicator as to how we are doing spiritually. When we are going through troubled times, we need to remember this scripture. In Psalm 30:5, David says, "For his anger endureth but a moment; in his favour is life: weeping may endure for a night, but joy cometh in the morning." The world does not have to be in turmoil. What we need is a way to conquer all the trials and temptations of life. Brother James tells us that there is a way to conquer all the trials. The Greek word for trials is *piras mos* which means to tempt, to try, to test, to prove, to be stronger. So then, the trials and temptations of life are to prove us. They are to test us and they serve a beneficial purpose in life.

What is the purpose of trouble? It will make us wiser and stronger. We will become a much purer and righteous person, a much stronger Christian; more steadfast and a better witness for the Lord. We will demonstrate the living presence and power of our Lord Jesus in us. So, when trouble comes, it is for our benefit. Troubles are to help us be more like Jesus.

Our primary goal in life is to be more Christlike. If God is going to mold us, fill us, and use us, He has to allow us to go through some things like Jesus went through. God never intended for us to stop growing, but to become a sanctuary tried and true. We are to reflect more of His glory. Sometimes, we feel that we have reached a place of perfection and no longer have a need to grow or grow stronger in our Christian lives. When this happens, God will allow adversity to come into our lives to move us forward in our daily walk with Him. This causes us to grow more mature. How we respond to our trials will either mold us or break us.

Why is it that when we encounter trouble, trials, and adversity, we want to quit church? Some quit serving God while others quit reading the Bible just because of troubles. There are some who become angry and bitter with God because of their troubles; as though God has done them injustice. Many have expressed that God has been unfair to them. James 1:3 and 4 says, "Knowing this, that the trying of your faith worketh patience. But let patience have her perfect work, that ye may be perfect and entire, wanting nothing." Isn't it good to know that the troubles we are facing and the problems that we are encountering have a purpose for us? Paul says, in Romans 8:28, "And we know that all things work together for good to them that love God, to them who are the called according to his purpose." Say this with me, "I am called. You are called. We are called."

We are going through this for a reason. We can make it and we will count it all joy! Know this is only a test. God is doing something in our lives to refine our walk with Him. We need to know that trials and troubles will purify us. Hebrew 10:38 says, "Now the just shall live by faith: but if any man draw back, my soul shall have no pleasure in him..." It is our faith which is being tried. Satan is being annoyed by it. He storms our faith. He attacks us, but he stumbles through our clear shield of faith. Our faith is tried and tested through many trials and temptations in life. Faith allows us to keep on going. Faith is a shield. It is a home grown fruit from the New Jerusalem. It is a gift from God from heaven. With this faith, we will trust God in the shadows as well as in the sunshine. Because your faith can see the sunshine in spite of the clouds, you can see the blessings in spite of the burdens, your reward in spite of the trials. When there is no way, faith will make a way. When there is no hope, faith will bring joy. When there is weakness, faith will bring strength. Faith will bring more fruits: blessing and assurance.

Remember sin is not the answer. Jesus Christ is the answer! So, ask your petition right now, because your guardian angel is starting to work on your behalf. In the sound of our voices, they are responding to our needs and it is not only one, but several of them. "And one angel took the censer and filled it with the prayers and petitions and filled it with fire from the altar and the smoke of the incense which came from the prayers of the people ascended up before God out of the angel's hands. And the angel with the censer flew around the throne of God who smelled the sweet incense of prayers from His saints. And He heard our voices singing, "Blessed assurance, Jesus is mine!"

Worship Planning Helps #5

"Blessed is the man that walketh not in the counsel of the ungodly, nor standeth in the way of sinners, nor sitteth in the seat of the scornful."
– Psalm 1:1

WELCOME:

On this beautiful Sunday, we happily recognize your presence at worship. Let the beatitudes of Jesus speak to all of us. Blessed are they which do hunger and thirst after righteousness, for they shall be filled.

INVOCATION:

God of Blessings,

How blessed we are when You dwell with us. Come now, in this time of worship and throughout the week. Strengthen us as we praise and pray that we may do more than recite the beatitudes, but live them, as well. As we joyfully come into Your house, may we also share the joyful burden of discipleship, living after the manner of Jesus, presenting the face of Jesus to the world. May we, strengthened by Your presence, become the face of Christ to those who are lost. May we become the hands of Jesus for those reaching out in sorrow. May our arms, open wide in welcome, become for those who are struggling a sure sign that You are here. These things we pray in Jesus' name. Amen.

OFFERING PRAYER:

Creator God,

You provide us with all we need for life. You nourish us like water nourishes a tree. We now share the fruit we have born as a result of our trust in You. Please accept our tithes and offerings as evidence that we trust in You always. Amen.

PRAYER FOR THE FAMILY OF GOD:

In the name of Jesus Christ, we come before Your throne, Father God. We come because we know You are all we need and You alone show us the way to a blessed life. We thank You for Your loving kindness and Your mercy toward us. We seek Your forgiveness for wandering from Your ways and walking in paths that do not lead us to blessedness, but to destruction. Teach us, Lord, to truly seek to live our lives in submission to You and to follow the paths that You have opened for us. Help us to understand that living in Your way means we must turn from the ways of the world. Instruct us and strengthen us to respond to life in the way You have spoken. Change our attitudes to be Your attitudes. Change our ways to become Your ways. You have declared that our blessings come only when we are surrendered to Your way of thinking and being. So, Lord, here we are. Change us, rearrange us, and empower us to become people who live by Your beatitudes. For in following Your ways, we will find the blessings of life that come from Your righteous hand. Amen.

BENEDICTION:
May God's promises reign in your hearts as you go forward from this place, rededicating your life to God, each and every day. Keep in mind God's beatitudes in all you do. Amen.

SUGGESTED HYMNS:
"Holy, Holy, Holy"
"Living for Jesus"
"Here I Am, Lord"
"Sanctuary"
"Trust and Obey"

Sermon #5:
"Jesus' Beatitudes"

Psalm 1, Psalm 15:1-5, Matthew 5:1-12

The beatitudes are very familiar to us. We have heard them many times. In fact, Jesus uses many different ways to get His point across to us. So, let's listen to this sermon on the Beatitudes and take Peter's advice.

There were once two men, Peter and Joe, who were out sailing in a boat when a thunder storm came in. Rain splashed down with strong winds. The waves were rocking the boat. They desperately moved from side to side to keep the boat from sinking. Peter shouted above the noisy storm, "It's times like this, I really wish I had listened to what my mom said." "Why?" asked Joe, "What did she say?" "I don't know," replied Peter, "I didn't listen!"

It could be frustrating and dangerous when we don't listen to God. That's why we need to listen to what Jesus says about our attitudes in life.

In today's Scripture, Jesus goes from a Galilean synagogue to Mount Tabor. This is where He preached His sermon on the Beatitudes. Jesus' choice of the mountain was to show the Pharisees who He was. Moses gave the law of God on the holy Mount of Sinai. But, there were other holy mountains, too: Mount Zion, Mount Moriah, the Mount of Olives, Mount Hermon, and Mount Precipos. Mount Tabor was a prophecy being fulfilled. In Jeremiah 46:18, we read, "As I live, says the king, whose name is the Lord of hosts, the Lord of the Sabbaoth, surely as Tabor is among the mountains, and as Carmel by the sea, so shall He come." No one was familiar with this prophecy. The disciples were not even equipped for their ministry. Can you imagine the questions they must have had? Can you hear Peter asking, "Do we have to write all this, Lord?" Or Andrew asking, "Are we supposed to know all of this stuff?" Or James asking, "Will we be tested on this, Lord?" Or Philip asking, "What if we don't know it all?" Or John saying, "The other disciples didn't have to learn this." Or Matthew, "This is too much for me!" or Judas, "Can we earn some money with this, Lord?" And Luke, "I can't learn all of this, but I'll try." And he did. He recorded the Beatitudes, the best way he could. He quotes four of the Beatitudes and the rest he starts with a "Woe unto you." This was the way that the prophets would preach the Word when God wanted a message delivered to the people in the Old Testament. Listen to Luke 6:24-26: "But woe unto you that are rich! for ye have received your consolation. Woe unto you that are full! for ye shall hunger. Woe unto you that laugh now! for ye shall mourn and weep. Woe unto you, when all men shall speak well of you! for so did their fathers to the false prophets." Luke was really putting into practice the Old Testament Torah.

We need to listen to what the Lord is telling us in church. Revelation 2:7 states, "He that has an ear, let him hear what the Spirit says to the church." His love embraces us if we listen to the Spirit of God. In Revelation 1:3, John says, "Blessed is he that readeth, and they that hear the words of this prophecy, and keep those things which are written therein: for the time is at hand." Listening can be the most important thing that we do, today. We do what we believe and we believe in what we do. We are here for one purpose and that is to let the Word of God inform us; let the Word of God expand our understanding; and let the Word of God bless us with the source of values and beliefs. It is important to let the Word of God put us in touch with our eternal matters and to give us the blessing due to us, today. The Word of God is to be released in this church, today. So, let it do its work. Let us feel His presence and receive our strength for the week. In Psalm 107:20, Moses says, "He sent his word, and healed them, and delivered them from their destructions." This is why the Lord chose the Beatitudes to be preached here, today, to receive His Word. "So shall my word be that goeth forth out of my mouth: it shall not return unto me void, but it shall accomplish that which I please, and it shall prosper in the thing whereto I sent it." (Isaiah 55:11) The blessing goes out to you. Let's claim them because we demonstrate: "Blessed are the poor in spirit: for theirs is the kingdom of heaven. Blessed are they that mourn: for they shall be comforted. Blessed are the meek: for they shall inherit the earth. Blessed are they which do hunger and thirst after righteousness: for they shall be filled. Blessed are the merciful: for they shall obtain mercy. Blessed are the pure in heart: for they shall see God. Blessed are the peacemakers: for they shall be called the children of God. Blessed are they which are persecuted for righteousness' sake: for theirs is the kingdom of heaven. Blessed are ye, when men shall revile you, and persecute you, and shall say all manner of evil against you falsely, for my sake. Rejoice, and be exceeding glad: for great is your reward in heaven: for so persecuted they the prophets which were before you." (Matthew 5:3-12) We will be fed for we will rejoice, for we will receive mercy, for we will leap with joy, for great is our reward in heaven.

So now, what we need are more members who will love the church. There is a blessing for those who love the church the way Christ loves it. I say, "Blessed is the church member who gives his church her rightful, loving affection. Blessed is the person who gives his church his loyal allegiance. Blessed is the Christian who gives his church his faithful attendance."

Let's look at the Beatitudes: **"Blessed are the poor in spirit."** This is not referring to the Christian with his head drooped and the pressures of the world upon him. In fact, it means poor in ego. But, if we empty ourselves, then there is room for God to fill us with His blessings. When Jesus preached these Beatitudes, the audience consisted of poor people who desired material goods. So, being poor in spirit was a blessing.

"Blessed are the merciful." Mercy often refers to showing kindness to the unfortunate and pity to the needy. Jesus' act of mercy occurred on the cross while praying, "Father, forgive them for they know not what they do." So, please do not repay anyone evil for evil. Instead, do right in the eyes of God and you will be rewarded for doing good.

"Blessed are the peacemakers." "If it be possible, as much as lieth in you, live peaceably with all men." Paul writes to the Romans (14:13). "Let us not therefore judge one another any more: but judge this rather, that no man put a stumblingblock or an occasion to fall in his brother's way." (Romans 14:13) Paul also writes to the Galatians and says, "Be not deceived; God is not mocked: for whatsoever a man soweth, that shall he also reap." (Galatians 6:7)

"Blessed are the pure in heart." To be pure in heart is to be holy and to see Jesus is to know the meaning of true blessedness. Jesus said, "I am the way, the truth, and the life: no man cometh unto the Father, but by me. If ye had known me, ye should have known my Father also: and from henceforth ye know him, and have seen him." To be pure in heart means that one approaches God with no ifs, no buts, or maybes. Paul says, "And be not conformed to this world: but be ye transformed by the renewing of your mind, that ye may prove what is that good, and acceptable, and perfect, will of God" (Romans 12:2)

"Blessed are the meek." Contrary to some people's belief, meekness is not weakness. Basically, being meek is placing one's will in line with God's will. Paul says, in Romans 12:9, "Let love be without dissimulation. Abhor that which is evil; cleave to that which is good." So, we must pick and choose how we will react to the things we encounter every day.

A Sunday school teacher asked her young scholars if anyone could tell the class what the Beatitudes are. While the rest of the class thought about it, little Suzy raised her hand in excitement, fairly bursting with the answer. "Oh, teacher, I know, I know, I know!" "Okay," said the teacher, "tell us." Suzy exclaimed, "The Beatitudes are the attitudes we ought to be at!" How true! Yes, we should be more like Jesus.

When Matthew wrote, **"Blessed are those who mourn"**, he was referring to a Christian solution to trials. Trouble is not a punishment, but an opportunity; a chance to build a life after the pattern of Jesus who was made perfect through suffering. Paul says, in II Corinthians 1:3 & 4, "Blessed be God, even the Father of our Lord Jesus Christ, the Father of mercies, and the God of all comfort; Who comforteth us in all our tribulation, that we may be able to comfort them which are in any trouble, by the comfort wherewith we ourselves are comforted of God." Just as Christ shares our burdens, we ought to share one another's burdens, too.

"Blessed are those who hunger and thirst after righteousness." In other words, God is only found by those who desire Him. God mentions the craving for Him as a hunger and thirst because it is the best way. The world seeks pleasure, fame, money, power, but not righteousness. To hunger and thirst after righteousness means that its fulfillment does not depend upon worldly circumstances. Nothing can beat you out of your desires. Paul says, in Romans 14:13, "For whether we live, we live unto the Lord; and whether we die, we die unto the Lord: whether we live therefore, or die, we are the Lord's."

So, the Sermon on the Mount is a trustworthy guide for us. Each of us should urgently examine ourselves against it and with God's help, re-establish a strong and loving relationship with Jesus. We must humbly submit to God in obedience to the Sermon's instructions. Then, we can be assured we will not be worldly and God will restore us to a unity far better than we have ever had before with Jesus' Beatitudes. Amen.

Worship Planning Helps #6

"And I John saw the holy city, new Jerusalem, coming down from God out of heaven, prepared as a bride adorned for her husband."
– Revelation 21:2

WELCOME:
Good morning and greetings in the name of our Lord and Savior Jesus Christ. To God be the glory, today and always. Amen!

INVOCATION:
Eternal Father,
You have promised that, one day, we will dwell with You in Heaven. But, You also promised that You would be in the midst of Your people as we gather to praise and worship You. Grant to us hearts of eager anticipation and expectation to be in Your presence. May we find renewed hope and joy as we wait for You. Amen.

OFFERING PRAYER:
We offer ourselves to You, O God, that we may be transformed into Your servants and Your ministers to this world. We offer our gifts that they may be used to spread Your gospel throughout all creation. Amen.

PRAYER FOR THE FAMILY OF GOD:
Glorious God,
We pray with the writer of the letter to the seven churches of Revelation. "Blessed are they that read and they that hear the words of this prophecy and keep those things which are written therein; for the time is at hand." Give us a spirit of wisdom and revelation as we grow in You. Enlighten the eyes of our hearts. Teach us the hope to which You call us. Show us the riches of the inheritance of the saints and the greatness of Your power. Enable us to see Your work in the world and to join You by doing Your will. Draw us into Your body, the church, that we might know the fullness of Your love and grace.

Lord, we bring to You this prayer and this morning's petitions. O Lord, hear our prayer and answer these petitions for our brothers and sisters in the Lord. They have come with tender hearts and humble spirits and You will not forsake. You tell us in Your Holy Word to pray for others and to agree together. "Weep with those who weep and rejoice with those who rejoice." Bless these prayers that come before Your glorious throne of mercy and of grace. Your word, Jesus, is the power of God and our words have power to influence and Your blessing has power to save Your children from their problems. You have said,

"Whatsoever things you desire, when you pray, believe that you receive them, and you shall have them."

This is Your house and it is called the house of prayer. It is not by might nor by power, but by Your Holy Spirit, O Lord. I pray for the congregation, this morning. May Your blessings be upon them, their homes, and their families. Set their hearts right before You. "Give them life and life more abundant."

Lord, we love You and adore You. We lift up Your holy name, Jesus Christ, so You may draw us unto You. For Your whole earth will be filled with Your glory and Your whole earth will be filled with Your knowledge. All the glory and honor and power are Yours forevermore. Thank You, Lord, for having Your ears open unto our prayer and for having Your eyes upon us. In Jesus' name, Amen.

BENEDICTION:

Go out into the world as God's people. Grow in God's kingdom and invite others to join the journey. Let us move forward in our faith and in our ministry through the power of Jesus Christ who goes before us. Amen.

SUGGESTED HYMNS:

"This World Is Not My Home"
"When the Roll Is Called Up Yonder"
"Sweet By and By"
"When We All Get to Heaven"
"In the Presence of Jehovah"
"Holy Ground"
"Mansion Over the Hilltop"

Sermon #6:
"Our New Home"

Isaiah 65:17–25 & Revelation 21:1–14

What will Heaven be like? What will it be like to live with God forever? We would want to live in a world where all the bad things of this world are going to be destroyed. All the problems, pollution, profane, destruction, suffering and pain, all impurities and corruption and death will vanish. We want to live in a world where there are no more bad leaders, bad law enforcements, or false doctrine. No more sin or temptation. That's the message for this morning. Revelation portrays a glorious message.

God is going to take Satan and all the ungodliness of this world and destroy them. God is going to create a new heaven and a new earth. All things will become new. Revelation 21 describes what this new world will be like. It gives us a sneak preview. The sky and earth, as we know it, are going to pass away. Everything is going to be destroyed and everything is going to be new.

For those of you who think that this sounds bizarre, have you considered the world's stock of weapons lately? In Revelation, Jesus says, that the sky, the sun, moon, stars, and planets are going to be destroyed. There will be no more violent thunder storms, tornadoes, typhoons, hurricanes, or destructive weather patterns.

God is going to make a new heaven. Think how beautiful the heavens look now when we look up on a clear night. Then, imagine what they will be like when God recreates them with all the glory and majesty of a perfect universe, a place where nothing burns out or wears out or dies. Everything will reflect the glory and splendor of God. The heavenly bodies will look the same as our earthly bodies. But with the light of God's glory, we will receive its power to stay young and will receive the strength from His Spirit to be big and strong and healthy. Now, if you can't imagine this, don't worry. It is beyond our human minds.

But, rest assured, there is going to be a new earth. The present earth is defective. It is cursed by so many drug dealers, cartels, gangs, killings, lies, bad language, earth quakes, floods, scorching heat, freezing winters, famines, disease, and death. God is going to destroy all of this. When? During the third war, God is going to replace the earth with a new world. The Word says that, "Ye are of God, little children, and have overcome them: because greater is he that is in you, than he that is in the world." (I John 4:4) We will win the battle. No more disasters or destruction. No more thorns or thistles. No more hunger or thirst. No more decay or erosion. The new earth will flourish and be fruitful; bearing all the good things that can be imagined. Think how beautiful, green and flourishing, blooming and productive and fruitful it will be. Think how peaceful and free, how easy and comfortable it will be when the Lord we shall see. Think of the security and provision, the abundance and overflowing of every good and perfect gift, the fullness of life that will be possible upon this new earth.

Imagine the new world, the New Jerusalem, coming down from heaven, prepared as a bride adorned for her husband. Revelation also reveals that "there was no more sea." There will be no gulf between God and people; no division between Glory and the new earth. A perfect earth is beyond our comprehension. But, it is exactly what the Scripture says is going to happen. "But the day of the Lord will come as a thief in the night; in the which the heavens shall pass away with a great noise, and the elements shall melt with fervent heat, the earth also and the works that are therein shall be burned up. Seeing then that all these things shall be dissolved, what manner of persons ought ye to be in all holy conversation and godliness." (II Peter 3:10-11)

Revelation promises that there will be a new city of God, the New Jerusalem. The idea is that the New Jerusalem will be the capital city in the new earth. It will be the place where God will be in human flesh as He was revealed in the Old Testament through "Jeshua" which means the Lord is salvation. He was not a stranger to Abraham or Sarah or Hagar or to Isaiah and the prophets of the Old Testament. God's presence will be manifested everywhere in all of His glory and majesty. The Holy City will give believers a place with which to identify as they serve God throughout the universe. In the New Jerusalem, they will have the tabernacle where God will rule and require His believers to occasionally visit and report to their work. Our Scripture says it will be as beautifully prepared as a bride is for her husband. This is the New Jerusalem!

Remember, Jesus Christ told His disciples that He was going away to prepare a place for them. It will be a place of fellowship with Jesus Christ and the Holy Spirit. God has set up the temple right there in the new mansion, our new worship center, a place where the very presence and glory of Jesus will dwell in a very special way. People will never again be able to remove God's presence among them. Sober people long for the presence of God and reasonable people long for the glory and fullness of a life with God.

Did I say sober people? I meant to say SAVED people. Most of the people have yet to discover that their hearts long for God. People try to fill their hearts' desire with worldly pleasures and possessions, but nothing satisfies them except God's Spirit. People, who refuse to allow God to fill their hearts, go through all kinds of negative experiences; lack of purpose, meaning, and significance; emptiness, questioning and wondering about life; routine and draining lives; insecurity and fear and failure. But, when people give their lives to God, they begin to fellowship with God and to experience all the fullness of life. People will never be without the presence and glory of God.

In Revelation 21:3 John says, "And I heard a great voice out of heaven saying, Behold, the tabernacle of God is with men, and he will dwell with them, and they shall be his people, and God himself shall be with them, and be their God." Think how wonderful it will be! We will be able to talk and share with God, face to face, when He calls us to His office or when we go to visit the New Jerusalem, with Jesus as our guide. God is going to take over the management of our lives throughout eternity. We shall serve and work for God in the New Jerusalem or in the new mansion. We shall be under His control and under His presence.

It is our NEW HOME! Life will be perfect. It will be totally different from what we now experience. The very life and vision people have longed for will become a living existence. All the suffering and evil of life, all the bad and negative experiences of life will be gone. "God shall wipe away all tears from our eyes." God will make us cry all our tears out on our judgment day, and we will go into this new heaven without any tears left. There will be no more miscarriages or dying children; no more dying mothers or fathers; no more funerals or cemeteries. Everyone will have a glorified body; a body that will be perfect, made incorruptible and immortal, perfect in strength and honor. There will be no more brokenness, regret, guilt, failure, or weakness. . There will be nothing to make us sorrowful. We will be capable and able, successful and fruitful, confident and secure. No more of anything that causes pain of any kind. Why? "Because the former things are passed away." (Revelation 21:4)

In I Corinthians 15:26 Paul says, "The last enemy that shall be destroyed is death." In Isaiah 65:19, we read, "And I will rejoice in Jerusalem, and joy in my people: and the voice of weeping shall be no more heard in her, nor the voice of crying." Can God say it any clearer? Revelation 21:5 says, "And he that sat upon the throne said, Behold, I make all things new." How? God declares, "I am Alpha and Omega, the beginning and the end, the first and the last." (Revelation 21:13) Alpha is the first letter in the Greek alphabet and it means "beginning". Omega is the last letter and it means "end". God is declaring that He is the beginning of all things and the end of all things.

Now, who will be the people of the new earth and the new heaven? Well, not everyone will live in the New Jerusalem; the Old Testament people work there and all who work outside. But, God makes sure we are acceptable to Him. God will give the water of life to all those who thirst after righteousness. Those who thirst after life; who desire the life that God wants people to live; the life that God gives; the fullness of life that is in God; the hope of life that God has planned for people; the perfection of life that God longs for people to live; to live and let people live! In the new heaven are those who work inside buildings and thirst after God; those who desire to fellowship and share life with God, who know salvation and forgiveness; those who know the hope and assurance and security of God; who live for God and obey and follow Him.

Now, who will not become a citizen of heaven? Heaven is not for those who do not thirst after God; who do not attend church where we can come before the throne of God. They do not confess or repent; or accept the gift of God's only Son. They do not fellowship and are not baptized. They do not take part in the Lord's Supper. They do not ask for mercy. They are not redeemed by Jesus' blood and they do not receive His Spirit. They are not transformed by His power. In Revelation 21:8 John says, "But the fearful, and unbelieving, and the abominable, and murderers, and whoremongers, and sorcerers, and idolaters, and all liars, shall have their part in the lake which burneth with fire and brimstone: which is the second death."

Are you forgiven; redeemed by His blood; saved by His Spirit and transformed by His power? Then, and only then, can we say, "I've got my pearly door open to God's heavenly kingdom!" If you are not redeemed, please repeat this prayer after me: Dear Lord Jesus, I come before You and ask You to cleanse me of all unrighteousness that I may confess You, Jesus Christ as Lord of my life. Right now, I accept You in my heart. I want to live for You from now on. Thank you, Jesus. Amen Church, amen!

Worship Planning Helps #7

"Blessed be the God and Father of our Lord Jesus Christ, which according to his abundant mercy hath begotten us again unto a lively hope by the resurrection of Jesus Christ from the dead."
– I Peter 1:3b

WELCOME:

We extend a warm welcome to all who have come to worship together. In spirit and in truth, let us worship Christ Jesus who died for us that we might live for Him!

INVOCATION:

God of my Salvation,

How I rejoice in You, for You are the Rock of my Salvation! You are my strength and my hope! May the words I speak and the thoughts I think show respect and reverence for You. As I bow before You in worship, draw near, O Lord, that I might sing of the wonders of Your love and rejoice in Your mercies and unfailing kindness. In Jesus' name, I pray. Amen.

OFFERING PRAYER:

We offer unto You, O God, our praises, our lives and our gifts. Receive and bless them so that Your reign might fully come on earth as in heaven. May the words of our mouths, the devotion of our hearts, and the hope of our lives all speak Your praises. Amen.

PRAYER FOR THE FAMILY OF GOD:

In the name of Jesus Christ, we come before Your glorious throne and bow before You, O God of all creation, because of Your awesome power and constant love. We see in our own bodies how bountiful is Your care. You have given us the ability to hear the sweet sounds of nature and the loving words of our friends. You have given us the gift of blessing, both to receive it and to give it. You are indeed a God of graciousness.

Lord, You have shown so much love and care in creating all that exists that it is in confidence we offer up to You those who are on our hearts. We know that You care for us and desire to hear those things that touch our lives. We know that You also care for those who are hurting in this church. We lift up to You those of this congregation, those of our families and friends who do not worship with us, those who we hear about in the news, and those whose pain is known only to You. As You minister to them in their need, soften our hearts that we may reach out to our neighbors in their troubles, also.

Bless us with wisdom, knowledge, and understanding of Your Word, in Jesus' name, as we lift our voices in prayer. Amen.

BENEDICTION:

The God who blesses you, this day, sends you out into the world to bless those you encounter. As you speak the words of peace, love, and hope to others, you will find your life filled with these, also. Go with God and be the blessing of God to others, this week. Amen.

SUGGESTED HYMNS:

"Since Jesus Came Into My Heart"
"How Great Thou Art"
"I Will Sing the Wondrous Story"
"The Solid Rock"
"Rock of Ages"
"Blessed Assurance"

Sermon #7:
"Are You Fanning Your Flame?"

Joel 2:28-32; Acts 2:14-33; I Peter 1:1-12

William Bradbury says, "My hope is built on nothing less than Jesus' blood and righteousness." Our hope is in the knowledge that the Lord has promised and secured this new life for us. If we persevere to the end, we will receive our reward. We live with the knowledge that God is our source of hope. Are you fanning your flame?

The apostle Peter says, "His boundless mercy that has given us the privilege of being born again, so that we are now members of God's family and is now the inheritance of our hope." But, we have to be in church in order to keep this hope in God. It doesn't work to put others before God. That's what the Bible says. We have to strive to be in church.

I have always read the King James Bible, and I love it. I fan my flame by reading the Word of God. But, this reading is a modern translation. It is the New Living Bible. The Scripture text we are about to study is about the hope of our Christian walk. It is important that those who still are babies in Christ and those who have been fooled by the lies and accusations of a cruel world will be encouraged to hold on and keep looking up with excitement for the return of our Lord Jesus Christ. We don't know when He is going to call us. Listen to this reading from I Peter 1:1-12.

What a beautiful passage of Scripture; it would take an eternity to grasp all that these verses teach us. Represented in these living words is the glorious hope of the return of our Lord Jesus Christ. In these living words is the great hope of every believer. It should be, for eternal life is the wonderful privilege of living forever with God.

Just imagine being able to float to God to give Him a big hug, every morning. I say, "Every morning," because it looks and feels like morning all day long in heaven; being able to see God, face to face, forever. There is no greater joy given to us.

This living hope is not a lifeless or dead hope. It is a hope that overcomes the grave; not a 'maybe' hope, but a hope that is real and true, a hope that really exists. As a believer in Jesus Christ, the reality of heaven is in your heart. What an honor I have to explain heaven to you. Listen to what the minor prophet Joel prophesied in Joel 2:28-32. Now, Peter uses it to defend the hope in his message recorded in Acts 2:14-33.

When we were younger, we hoped for lots of things. But, when we became Christian adults, our hope took on a new dimension. We put childish things away. We began to hope for things that the carnal world cannot see. Things like satisfaction, salvation, sanctification, and holiness. Therefore, if God is the source of our inheritance and the assurance of our hope, why then do so many Christians live, today, as those who have no hope? If Jesus Christ is our Lord, the One to whom we have surrendered and submitted our lives to, the One who sits in the spiritual and heavenly world at the right hand of God our Father, making intercession for us twenty-four hours a day; if He is our Messiah, promised by God to save the souls of people, then why is there a lack in fanning their own flame?

Some people are too busy gossiping and putting people down. It has become a bad habit. But, you know what God told me? He told me that He will take their pastor away from their church.

Peter's text comes to the doubting Christian. The Word of God comes to the one who is fanning the flame of his own faith. It re-ignites the hope that is in us; the hope that God has promised us eternal life if we only believe. Peter helps us fan the flame of our faith with some very simple truths.

First, he helps us fan our flame with the knowledge that God is not far from us. God is near, all around us, living within the spiritual world, and longing to relate to us and look after us and give us eternal life through His Son. He proved that He has the power to grant us eternal life for we have the record of Jesus Christ's resurrection and ascension as concrete proof that God will deliver us. Are you fanning your flame, now?

Peter fans our flame by warning us that we live in a world full of corruption and God is able to preserve us until His second coming. Even while we are here on earth among sin, shame, accident, disease, suffering, evil cursing, lying, accusations, stealing, deception, assaults, murders, and wars that engulf the earth, just like hell itself, God is able to stop the process of corruption and death by His mercy. In a world of sin, God is our only hope for redemption and rewards. Though people have mistreated their Creator, God has not forsaken us for His mercy endures forever. "But the mercy of the Lord is from everlasting to everlasting upon them that fear him, and his righteousness unto children's children." (Psalm 103:17) Are you fanning your flame with God's mercy?

From David's Psalm, Peter fans our flame by reminding us of our new Christian birth. Don't let anyone plant corrupted seeds in your new life. That is the old person in you; the one who rejected and rebelled against Christians and God. Peter reminds us that through our faith, we have been born anew. The sinful person is dead and we are now alive in Jesus Christ who has taken up residence in our hearts. This new body is part of our living hope for we are living a new life. "That which is born of the flesh is flesh; and that which is born of the Spirit is spirit." (John 3:6) "Therefore if any man be in Christ, he is a new creature: old things are passed away; behold, all things are become new." (II Corinthians 5:17) Are you fanning your flame with your new soul, body, and spirit?

Peter starts fanning our flame of faith with the assurance of the resurrection. As Jesus has been raised from the dead to live forever in heaven with His father, so shall we who are believers in Him! Jesus' resurrection from the dead assures us that God is able, that Jesus is who He claims to be, and we can be victorious over sin while we serve the Lord upon this earth. So, are you fanning your flame with the faith in resurrection?

Or what will it take to fan your flame, to cause a spiritual awakening in your soul, to feel the heat of God's promise, to know that you know that Jesus who has been raised from the dead will surely appear before us when we pass from this life to the next? Are you fanning the flame of your spiritual life, now?

We are adopted sons and daughters of God. We shall stand before our Creator. Then, we shall receive the gift of eternal life. We shall receive a new and glorious body. We will be given eternal rest and peace. We will receive the blessings of the Lord. We will come into the full knowledge of Jesus Christ. We will receive riches and blessings; the mercy of our God, the grace of our Lord Jesus Christ, a reward for our conversion, the cost of our redemption, the proof of our pardon, the funds of our commitment, and a great reward for being in church, every Sunday, the glory of our future. Revelation 22:14 says, "Blessed are they that do his commandments, that they may have right to the tree of life, and may enter in through the gates into the city." Some will have the opportunity to experience priesthood. But, no one comes before the King without a gift. So, we will receive crowns to offer the King; a crown of glory to offer to God and a crown of righteousness to offer our Lord Jesus Christ, and a crown of incorruption to show every eye that we overcame all false witnesses against us, a crown of life to wear proudly before the King of kings, and a crown of joy to wear before all of our loved ones there. We will all be united before His throne and reign together with Jesus and God forever and ever. Amen!

Worship Planning Helps #8

"Thy word is a lamp unto my feet, and a light unto my path."
– Psalm 119:105

WELCOME:

We extend a warm welcome to all who have come to worship together. May we seek to know the Word of God and the God of the Word that we might be transformed and conformed to the image of His Son, Jesus.

INVOCATION:

Father,

May Your Word, shown among us by those who speak, those who sing, those who lead, those who serve, those who wait, those who act, those who dream, and those who hope, bear fruit a hundredfold. May we take root and grow richly, sheltering and nurturing each other, safe against every storm. God, found in parable and known by all who hear, bless our time of worship, today. In Jesus' name, Amen.

OFFERING PRAYER:

We offer up to Thee, O God, these gifts as tokens of our devotion to You and as signs that we look to You, and not to material goods, for the fullness of our lives. Amen.

PRAYER FOR THE FAMILY OF GOD:

We worship and adore You, God of all creation, through Your Son, Jesus Christ, for You hold in Your hands all that is or ever will be. There is nothing that does not belong to You, including our very lives. We give You thanks for all the ways in which You have blessed us. We thank You for the abundance of creation and for the creativity that makes life easier for us all. We thank You for the inventors who find new ways to use Your gifts of creation. We thank You for Jesus who came and reminded us not to confuse the gift with the giver. Help us always to use Your gifts wisely and to not allow them to become idols in our lives. We know that a good share of Your children do not have a basic share of the good things You have given us. They do not have enough to eat or to wear, and they do not have adequate housing. As we enjoy what we have been blessed with, help us to remember that Jesus came and lived among us as one of the poor. Help us to focus our lives on You and to share the good things of this earth with others. As You reach out in love to those who are without, enlarge our hearts that we may give freely and joyously.

Lord, I pray for each one who is here, today, and I agree with their petitions. As I bring them before You, Lord, send Your word to heal and to glorify You. Heal those who need a healing touch from the Master's hand. Set Your eyes upon us and hear our prayers, O Lord our God, that we might be strengthened to serve You and to testify of Your work in our lives. Amen.

BENEDICTION:

Peace to the brethren and love with faith from God our Father and our Lord Jesus Christ. Grace be with you all who love the Lord. May You receive strength for Your victory, this week. In Jesus' name. Amen.

SUGGESTED HYMNS:

"Wonderful Words of Life"
"Standing on the Promises"
"Seek Ye First"
"Thy Word"

Sermon #8:
"Stand on the Word"

Psalm 19:7-14; Matthew 26:36-42; Ephesians 6:10-20

The Word of God assures us that the spiritual weapons which have been given unto us are for Christians to use to have the power to cast out demonic strongholds. In II Corinthians 10:4 & 5, Paul says, "For the weapons of our warfare are not carnal, but mighty through God to the pulling down of strong holds; Casting down imaginations, and every high thing that exalteth itself against the knowledge of God, and bringing into captivity every thought to the obedience of Christ." These are good weapons to memorize and to keep in mind when we are battling something that is bigger than we are that we cannot handle. In I Corinthians 10:13, Paul tells us, "There hath no temptation taken you but such as is common to man: but God is faithful, who will not suffer you to be tempted above that ye are able; but will with the temptation also make a way to escape, that ye may be able to bear it." To feel that relief, the Word assures us that these spiritual weapons demolish demonic strongholds. When the devil sends out his big forces, we can get out our big weapons, and in the name of the Lord, stand on the Word of God. It has the power to give us absolute victory and absolute triumph over demonic strongholds.

There is no stronghold too big for God to bring down. Isaiah 55:11 says, "So shall my word be that goeth forth out of my mouth: it shall not return unto me void, but it shall accomplish that which I please, and it shall prosper in the thing whereto I sent it." We can talk and walk in victory. Isaiah 55:12 declares, "For ye shall go out with joy, and be led forth with peace: the mountains and the hills shall break forth before you into singing, and all the trees of the field shall clap their hands!" You may say, "That sounds like a rosy picture, but it doesn't look like my life." Well, if you would go to church, every Sunday, it would. You know, Satan comes to kill, steal, and divide the church. Hopefully, these sermons centered upon spiritual warfare will help us to live in the victory that Jesus has provided for us.

How many of you know that there is a devil out there, because you have battled evil with him, a few times? We know that he is real. We may not face him, face to face, but we have most certainly experienced his influence and his impact. I wish there was a place of safety from him; and we do have such a place. We have to come to Jesus! We cannot flee and escape the devil's presence. Sometimes, it seems like everywhere we turn, there are the devil's footprints. There are times when we can even smell his filthiness and odor. But, remember this: do your best and God will do the rest. So, don't miss Sunday's church, because you will miss out on your blessings and everything you have will start falling apart.

So, why does the devil come around us, at work, at home, at dark hours, in the loneliness of night, in dreams, and in visions? Remember, we cannot walk on two roads with one foot on each road. We must have both feet on the narrow road with Jesus. We cannot turn to the right or to the left; we have to go straight up that narrow road to heaven. That is where Jesus is going to appear to us when we need Him the most. Thank God that we have four gospels and twenty-three epistles in the New Testament that tell us about Jesus Christ. Remember, we can't keep Satan off of the street, but we can keep him out of our house, because we belong to God and we are God's possession. James 4:7 says, "Submit yourselves therefore to God. Resist the devil, and he will flee from you." Paul says, in Ephesians 6:13, "Wherefore take unto you the whole armour of God, that ye may be able to withstand in the evil day, and having done all, to stand." Stand on the Word! Paul writes about this day as if it is a day that is on its way; a day that has been planned by Satan, a day which Satan has planned for our defeat and destruction, the day of evil that is beyond any normal day (if you have any normal days). There are some days when we can sense the devil's presence more than other times. That is one way the Holy Spirit warns us to be on guard and to walk carefully. We live in a world of evil and we confront evil every day. We need to be prepared.

In the Old Testament, King Uzziah was a godly king until one day sin entered into his heart and he transgressed against the Lord. That day, King Uzziah walked into the holy of holies, a place reserved for the priests only, and the Lord struck him with a disease that would change the rest of his life. The holy of holies is reserved for holiness and for God. King Uzziah went into the holy of holies, a sin in the eyes of God, and eighty other priests (four score) went in and forced him out. He lived the rest of his life in an isolated place and died of leprosy. Before that day, King Uzziah had been a good king. But, one day, Satan took him by surprise and he disobeyed the Lord. (II Chronicles 26)

King David was also taken by surprise, one night on his roof top. He committed lust, and then, he was unable to discipline himself. So, what happened next was an adulterous relationship with Bathsheba, murder, and lying; all sins that compromised the remainder of his reign as a king. That evil day had an effect upon David and his family forever. But, before that evil day, King David had been a man of integrity who trusted in the Lord; before Satan took him by surprise. Then, the Lord took everything he owned, even his life. Material things are not important to God if you put them before Him.

It is just like Ananias and Sapphira in the New Testament. They were saved and joined the church. But, in a moment of wanting exaltation, in a moment of wanting to be lifted up by the church, they lied about the amount of money they had been blessed with by the Lord. Then, they lied to the church and gave an offering based on their lie. Peter told them, "Thou hast not lied unto men, but unto God." And immediately, they fell to the ground dead. One evil day, Satan took them by surprise; and they lost everything.

In the Old Testament, a man named Samson was called by God to be a religious leader, one of the judges of Israel. He met a prostitute named Delilah. She moved into the neighborhood, and Samson looked upon her with lust, and his life fell apart. One day, he fell into a trap with her and committed sin. He disobeyed the Lord by not having his eyes on God but on Delilah. Not being in church will take your eyes away from God. One evil day, Satan took Samson by surprise.

And one evil day could change us forever, too, if we are in church and prepared. Or, it could change us for the worst and bring great spiritual disaster in our lives if we are not in church and prepared. If we are sick, God knows and understands. But, remember, it is a sin if we are not in church on worship day. We are instructed to "Not forsak[e] the assembling of ourselves together, as the manner of some is." Unless you are sick and cannot walk, you need to be in church! There are evil days planned for us and we need to know how to stand in those evil days.

I would like to share with you three things that we must do to be strong in the Lord and to be able to stand in the evil day. First, we must believe that we have a spiritual enemy, Satan, who has demonic spirits who are at his command. But, God has given His angels charge over you. The devil's purpose is to knock us down and knock us out of church. The devil has designed a plan especially for our weakness. But, God has a plan for us, also! It is when we least expect it that the devil comes at us the hardest. Attacks from the devil are going to happen so that you can miss worship. This is why we need to commit to and be dedicated to God and to the church.

Second, once we recognize the devil's plan, we must rise up against him by having Bible studies, worshipping in church, fearing God, and worshipping God as much as possible. We cannot defeat Satan in our own strength. It is God who helps us overcome the plans, the battles, and the temptations of the devil. When the Israelites crossed the Red Sea, they sang a song of praise unto the Lord. (Exodus 15:2,3) "The Lord is my strength and song, and he is become my salvation: he is my God, and I will prepare him an habitation; my father's God, and I will exalt him." In II Samuel 22:33, David says, "God is my strength and power: and he maketh my way perfect." In Psalms 18:2 & 3, David says, "The Lord is my rock, and my fortress, and my deliverer; my God, my strength, in whom I will trust; my buckler, and the horn of my salvation, and my high tower. I will call upon the Lord, who is worthy to be praised: so shall I be saved from mine enemies." In Psalms 27:1-5, David declares, "The Lord is my light and my salvation; whom shall I fear? the Lord is the strength of my life; of whom shall I be afraid?" In I Samuel 17:37, we read, "The Lord that delivered me out of the paw of the lion, and out of the paw of the bear, he will deliver me out of the hand of this Philistine. And Saul said unto David, Go, and the Lord be with thee." We need to know that the battle belongs to the Lord. He will either spare you from suffering or give you the grace to bear it in victory through Jesus Christ.

Third, we must resist daily struggles. Most of the time, we face the same temptation over and over. The devil doesn't give up easily. He is the prince of darkness and the prince of lies. The devil is a determined enemy. He will not give up on us. He will not give up on us until we get to heaven. So, we can't give up now, because heaven is just around the corner for us.

My temptations are different than yours. But, our armor is the same for our protection. The armor of God which is made up of our pants of truth, our hat of salvation, our shoes of peace, our breastplate of righteousness, our shield of faith which is clear to see through, and the sword of the Spirit which is the Word of God. When we use the armor, we are strong in the Lord and in His power and in His might. But, the choice is ours to put on the armor or not. The choice is ours to be prepared by reading God's Word and praying. The family of God is here to stand on the Word and to stand beside you. You are not alone. Call on the prayer chain. We will pray for you and anoint you with oil if you want us to. We claim our victory through faith in Jesus' name. Amen, church? Amen!

Worship Planning Helps #9

"Blessed are the pure in heart: for they shall see God."
– Matthew 5:8

WELCOME:
We extend a warm welcome to all who have come to worship. May we seek God through Jesus with all of our hearts that the thirst of our souls might be satisfied by Him.

INVOCATION:
Tender and compassionate God, in whose arms we are held, draw us to Yourself in love, surround us with Your grace, and keep us in the shelter of Your wings. Cleanse the thoughts of our hearts that we may perfectly love You and magnify Your holy name through Jesus Christ, our Lord. Amen.

OFFERING PRAYER:
We bring our gifts to You, O God, as a service of our love and the faithfulness of our lives to You. As You bless these offerings for ministry, bless us, also, that we may grow in faith and Your Word to share with others. Amen.

PRAYER FOR THE FAMILY OF GOD:
We bless and praise the God who made creation to grow and to become. The entire world is changing and growing into the fullness of its created potential. Seeds grow and mature into strong trees. Wobbly-legged colts become fleet racers. Newborn Christians grow into mature saints. For all these miracles, we offer praise to You O God. We pray a silent prayer of thanksgiving at this moment unto You, O Lord. The care You have shown in making a world that grows and develops shows us the love You have for all Your creatures. We have received Your grace and know You are offering it to all. So, we join Your great mission of love and lift up to You those who are hurting and lost. We remember those who are ill in body, mind, or spirit. We recall those who are homeless, hungry, and poor. We bring to You those who are victims of war, violence, famine, and political oppression. We lift up those who have lost their way in life. We pray for the new petitions that were shared, this morning, and we pray for the congregation, O Lord. Bless them and take care of them, this week, and bless their families. Heal them in any way that they need Your healing touch. You are our God, the same One as the Old Testament Rapha, our Lord the Healer. So, we put our trust in You and thank You for Your answers to our prayers. Amen.

BENEDICTION:

May the Lord walk beside you to comfort you. May the Lord keep His eyes upon you. May the Lord walk behind you to protect you. May the Lord walk before you to lead you through this coming week. Amen.

SUGGESTED HYMNS:

"Higher Ground"
"As the Deer"
"What a Friend We Have in Jesus"
"Lord, Prepare Me"
"Solid Rock"
"Faith is the Victory"

Sermon #9:
"Where Is Thy God?"

Psalm 42; Joel 2:12-17

With his request approved, the CNN news cameraman quickly used his cell phone to call the local airport to charter a flight. He was told a twin engine plane would be waiting for him at the airport. Arriving at the airfield, he spotted a plane warming up outside a shed. He jumped in with his bag, slammed the door shut, and shouted, "Let's go!" The pilot taxied out, swung the plane into the wind and took off. Once in the air, the cameraman instructed the pilot, "Fly over the valley and make low passes so I can get some shots of the fires on the hillsides." "Why?" asked the pilot. "Because, I'm a cameraman for CNN," he responded, "and I need to get some close-up shots." The pilot was silent for a moment. Finally, he mumbled, "You're not my flight instructor?"

We all have difficult times in our lives and being able to view God and hear His voice, too. It does not matter what spiritual level we are at; we all long for the renewal of God's divine presence. Yet, we are going through difficult times because of our doubts and fears in life. We know we have to live by faith and not by sight. "For therein is the righteousness of God revealed from faith to faith: as it is written, The just shall live by faith." (Romans 1:17) Yet, many still ask, "Where is thy God?" So, let's examine the Bible and look at the life of King David.

David is running from King Saul who is seeking to kill him. David is discouraged and going through a struggle like many of us have experienced in life. David, a king and a servant of the Lord God Almighty has been forced out of his kingdom and he feels he has no place to go. He misses the temple and he longs for the presence of God. But, God seems to be nowhere around. By now, everyone in his company is asking, "Where is thy God, David?" And that is the question: Where is our God when we need Him the most?

Let's examine, again, David's words that are recorded in the Bible. "As the hart panteth after the water brooks, so panteth my soul after thee, O God. My soul thirsteth for God, for the living God: when shall I come and appear before God?" (Psalm 42) David is comparing his thirst and hunger with a thirsty deer in danger in the wild. "When shall I come before God?" This is David's deepest desire; to experience and sense the Spirit of God. Let me ask you, this morning, are you thirsty for God? For His Word? For worship? Or, do we need a little more salt in our Christian diet? David had a beautiful sanctuary where he danced unto the Lord and played his harp. He worshipped the Lord in His sanctuary, pure and holy, tried and true. Then, the words come that reveal David's heart. "My tears have been my meat day and night, while they continually say unto me, Where is thy God." (Psalm 42:3) "Where is thy God, David?"

I believe this is a spiritual statement referring to a great abundance in David's life. David's tears and grief came before God and God took away David's very hunger. David was fasting. David's men were asking, "David, where is thy God?' This is a very important question: God, where are You? And, this is a very dangerous question, too. To tell you the truth, it is an ancient question. This question is asked by unbelievers, as well as believers, too. But, it penetrates the heart of the believer because of the Holy Scriptures. As we see David, crying out to God, his own men are staring at him and making fun of him, "Where is thy God, David? It appears that your God is gone and has departed from you. Remember, you used to dance before thy God…?" When David was in his castle, he would go down the hall with these men to the temple. He would teach his men the Law of Moses. But, when David's enemies would leave, David would bend his knee before Yahweh, our Divine Salvation, and cry out in prayer. "When I remember these things, I pour out my soul within me; for I had gone with the multitude, I went with them to the sanctuary of God, with the voice of joy and praise, with people that kept the holy days." David went to church just as a real, born again saint of God will want to go to church. David had visions of this Old Testament mansion God promised him in heaven; similar to the new mansion Jesus promises us in heaven.

In II Corinthians 12:2, Paul says that he was caught up to the third heaven. The first heaven is where God's throne is established and the Ark of the Covenant and all of His heavenly angels are. The second heaven is where the Old Testament mansion is, that Yahweh promised, where David appeared walking with the people that kept holy days. And, the third heaven is where Paul went to visit the New Testament mansion. "I knew a man in Christ above fourteen years ago, (whether in the body, I cannot tell; or whether out of the body, I cannot tell: God knoweth;) such an one caught up to the third heaven," Paul says. So, these are the three heavens Paul talked about.

Many Christians have had to pass through difficult times of great stress; often, we have looked at our tragedy and dreadful moments as though God is not there. Remember, the Word of God says, "Blessed are those who hunger and thirst after righteousness; for they will be fed." We will confess with our mouths that Jesus is Lord of our dreadful moments.

Moses wondered with his worried people as they journeyed to the Promised Land, "Are we there, yet? Are we there, yet?" Noah wondered with the troubled people, "Is it going to rain? Is it going to rain?" Elijah wondered about his servant, "Where is thy God? Is God going to rescue us?" Elijah had to pray for Yahweh to show his servant that God was their divine salvation. Jonah suffered in the belly of a fish for three days and three nights.

There was a Kindergartener who shared about Jonah, eaten by a fish and spending three days and three nights in the fish's belly. The teacher asked her, "Do you believe that?" "Oh, yes!" she said. "It's in the Bible. And when I go to heaven, I'll ask him." "And what if Jonah is not there?" the teacher asked. "Then, you ask him."

Our next scripture says, "Why art thou cast down, O my soul? And why are thou disquieted within me? Hope thou in God; for I shall yet praise Him for He has accepted me. O, my God, my soul is cast down within me; therefore, will I remember Thee." The words, 'cast down' mean to be humbled to the lowest degree. David commands his soul to have hope in Elohim, the God of Power. David knew that this creation gave proof that there is a God. God is the creator of all creation, the designer above all designers, and the law giver above all law givers. God stepped out from eternity into time. And now, He is always on time. But, David needed Him, right there and then. Sometimes, it is good to wait and see the salvation of the Lord. Job said we have to wait on the Lord. Isaiah said, "They that wait upon the Lord shall renew their strength." Micah said, "I will wait for the Lord of my salvation."

David continues in verse eight of Psalm 42:8, "Yet the Lord will command his lovingkindness in the day time, and in the night his song shall be with me, and my prayer unto the God of my life." Lovingkindness means mercy, goodness, or faithfulness. This is what God commands us to follow each day. When David received God's assurance of goodness, he prayed, "God is our refuge and strength, a very present help in trouble." Today, the Holy Spirit helps us to pray. Here, God shows David that God is the same, yesterday, today, and forever. He represents His name EL, God's great name which means Almighty God of Power, the God of Abraham, Jacob, and the apostles. Now, when David could not find good news, he produced some of his own. With an assurance of life, either on earth or in heaven, David is satisfied. Praise you the Lord!

Let's continue with verse ten: "As with a sword in my bones, mine enemies reproach me; while they say daily unto me, Where is thy God?" 'As with a sword in my bones' means David's enemies were continually after him. They hated him. These were serious and dangerous people. And what upset David the most was when his enemies would say, "Where is thy God?" We have all gone through difficulties. I have fallen down to my knees and shed tears. I have fought sin that has tried to conquer my body, soul, and spirit. But, the Lord has not allowed it to do so, because I carry a promise between the Lord and me that says, "I will never leave thee nor forsake thee, but I will always be with you."

Verse eleven. "Why art thou cast down, O my soul? and why art thou disquieted within me? hope thou in God: for I shall yet praise him, who is the health of my countenance, and my God." This verse is a repetition. So, I will just briefly go over it. David has matured some. Now, he commands his soul to praise God. God has helped David so that his face has begun to shine. Now, David calls God, "the health of his countenance". Now, he calls God, Yeshuah which means deliverance. But, look at David's trials and heartaches. They made God appear much closer and have made David truly trust his Heavenly Father. David has spent so much time with God that David's face changes. David has grown during his trials. And so will we, if we do what Psalm 119:71 says, "It is good for me that I have been afflicted; that I might learn thy statutes." I pray that you have received both a blessing and spiritual growth by reflecting on Psalm 42. Amen.

Worship Planning Helps #10

"But without faith it is impossible to please him: for he that cometh to God must believe that he is, and that he is a rewarder of them that diligently seek him."
– Hebrews 11:6

WELCOME:

We extend a warm welcome to all who have come to worship. In the presence of God, may we find the boldness and courage to faithfully proclaim His message of love and salvation.

INVOCATION:

Lord, often we have been so busy with the everyday matters of the world that we have neglected or even thought it not important enough to take the time to share the Good News of Your love with those around us. Forgive us, Lord, and help us to boldly share the wonderful news of Your love with our hearts. Amen.

OFFERING PRAYER:

Holy God, in Jesus' name, it is in fulfilling our vows unto Thee that we bring these gifts and offerings into Your house. Surely, You have been faithful to us for Thy grace is sufficient. May all that we do confess Your love and Your glory. Amen.

PRAYER FOR THE FAMILY OF GOD:

Dear Heavenly Father God, in the precious name of Your beloved Son, Jesus, we come before You. Precious Lord, there are times when we must acknowledge that our own strength and wisdom and resources are insufficient to meet the needs of those around us. The sicknesses are too advanced, the wounds are too deep, the agony is too intense, and the situations are too complicated. Our hearts and spirits long to reach out to fix and to heal, but we fall so very short. It is in these times, we must turn to You, Heavenly Father, for You see and You hear and You heal and make whole. You are our help and our hope and our strong right arm. We bow before You and lay at Your feet our brothers and sisters in need. Hear now our prayers. (Silent Prayer)

I pray for the petitions that are brought before Thee, this morning, O Lord from Your people. Bless them, Father God, in Jesus' name. I want to hear testimonies about Your wondrous glory. I want Your people to be blessed when they go into their homes and when they go out of their homes. Bless them with good health, this coming week. Bless their families, too. Take good care of them. I pray and agree together with them in one accord. For the hope, sufficiency and comfort of Your grace, we give You thanks. Amen.

BENEDICTION:

May the blessings of the Lord be upon you. I bless you in the name of the Lord Jesus Christ. May the fruit and gift of faith be with you, this coming week. Amen.

SUGGESTED HYMNS:

"I Love to Tell the Story"
"The Old Rugged Cross"
"Oh, How I Love Jesus"
"In His Time"
"Living for Jesus"

Sermon #10:
"Are You Excited About Jesus?"

Mark 2:1-12; Philippians 2:1-11

Dr. Norman Peale once told a story about a young man named James McCormick. He was stricken with polio. This was before the vaccine. James was paralyzed, totally helpless, and in pain. He could not move. He could not swallow. He could not breathe. He had to stay on a respirator. He wanted to die. He even prayed, "Lord, I am so helpless that I can't even take my own life. Please take it for me." Then, he prayed, "If I can't die, please take away this awful pain." Then, the doctor prescribed pain medication, but he was becoming dangerously dependent on them. He prayed, "Lord, please take away this craving for drugs." Gradually, the craving left him. Then, he prayed, "Please let me be able to swallow, again. Let them take this tube out of my throat and these needles out of my arms, and if I can just drink a little water, I'll try not to ask for any more favors." And he became able to swallow, but he was not able to stop asking God for favors. So, he prayed, "Lord, let me be able to breathe a little bit on my own. Let me be able to get off of this respirator just for a little while." And he did. After a while, he prayed again, "Heavenly Father, I am so grateful for all your favors. Can I ask for just one more? Let me be able to leave this bed, just for an hour; to get into a wheelchair, and see the world that lies outside this hospital room." This request was granted. Then, James asked to be given strength enough in his arms to move the wheelchair by himself. And after that, he asked for the strength to walk on crutches. And finally, after a twenty year struggle, James could walk with two canes. God blessed him because he had been a good man. Then, he met a lady and became friends. After a while, they married and had children. Jesus blessed him with a close to normal life. James took his family to church as he was once taught by his parents. James' prayers were answered, not the way he wanted them to be, but he had no doubt that Jesus heard his prayers and God shook His head yes. He never let go of the name of salvation.

And we, too, have to be sure that we have that name of salvation. That name is Jesus, Joshua, Yeshua, and Yahweh; all meaning divine salvation. All other names, Rapha heals, Jehovah creates, Eli my God, are the different names people used to describe God as He manifested Himself to them. Until Paul said, "Neither is there salvation in any other: for there is none other name under heaven given among men, whereby we must be saved." And the Lord told me that this is someone's prayer being answered, today! Someone needed to hear this.

And now, I want to share with you that nothing excites God more than to see His people live by faith in Jesus and in His Word and to take Him at His Word and act upon it. In these scriptures, we will find one of the most awesome miracles in the Bible. I am going to share three points that can get us to see these things taking place in our daily life.

First, God moves when we share Him with others. When Jesus entered into Capernaum, after some days, it spread throughout the area that Jesus was at Paul's house. Immediately, lots of people came by and filled the whole house. Jesus started preaching the Word to them. Then, four men came carrying a paralyzed man who wanted Jesus to heal him. He needed Jesus in his life and needed somebody to bring him to Jesus. Even if this man could have gotten to the house on his own, he couldn't have gotten in. That place was absolutely full and there was no room. All seats were taken and some people were standing. Besides, this man could not stand. It is heart breaking that all these men are trying to carry the paralyzed man into the house and no one would let them in. You see this crowd cared more about their seats than they did about the hurting person. They were more self-centered than they were people-centered. That old conscience says, "I care more about myself than I care about you." In John 15:12, Jesus says, "This is my commandment, That ye love one another, as I have loved you." I want to respectfully ask you to consider that every time we come to church, we ought to provide a manner that is most helpful to others to get to know Jesus. If a person who needs Jesus walks into this church, we want everything they see and hear to point them to Jesus. We want them to say, "These people really care about me."

The paralytic's biggest hindrance to getting to Jesus was the Scribes and the Pharisees. They didn't do anything to help this man get to Jesus. They didn't bring anyone to hear the gospel message. They were there to criticize and to say, "This man speaks blasphemies. Who can forgive sins, but God alone?" You know the greatest hindrances people have coming to church is not the atheist or the unbeliever, but the cold, calloused, critical, carnal person who, by their negative comments, gives a person every reason not to come to Jesus for help. I am convinced that, when you come to church and you ask Jesus for something, you are going to get exactly what you are looking for. But, in His time, all things become beautiful. If you want a blessing, you will know when it is coming. But, thank God for these four men who were willing to bring this paralyzed man to Jesus. These were servants and friends because you will never have a greater friend than the one who will serve you and bring you to the Master. You know why they did this? They brought their friend to Jesus because they cared and they wanted to see a miracle. The first step to sharing is caring. No matter how much you have, if you don't care, you won't share. These men cared enough about the paralyzed man to go and pick him up and bring him to Jesus. Remember when we didn't know the Lord and someone brought us to Jesus? Somebody cared for us; and the most beautiful blessing one could ever have eternally is to bring someone to church to hear God's Word so that they can meet Jesus. Salvation comes only through Jesus Christ and He is the only way to God; A through Z, Alpha and Omega, the Beginning and the End, Genesis through Revelation. God started the Bible and Jesus said, in John 19:30, "It is finished!" God closed the Old Testament and Jesus opened the

New Testament. We were dead in sin and Jesus gave us life; and life more abundantly. Why? Because Jesus cares! Because He cares for us!

Second, God gets excited when we use faith. When the men carrying the paralyzed man could not come near Jesus, because of the crowd, they went to the side of the house and up to the roof. There, they uncovered a section of the roof above where Jesus was. They let down the bed, on which the paralyzed man lay, right before Jesus. They had no other choice but to put their faith into practice and to see a miracle. Even though it was kind of dangerous, they still took the chance. They didn't care about criticism. They did not care about rejection. They did not care about the people or different denominations. They were determined to see a miracle. They knew Jesus could meet the need of their friend. And, they had the faith to do something about it! As James 2:26 says, "For as the body without the spirit is dead, so faith without works is dead also." Jesus saved this man, and then, he healed him. Jesus said, in Matthew 18:19, "Again I say unto you, That if two of you shall agree on earth as touching any thing that they shall ask, it shall be done for them of my Father which is in heaven."

It is nice to wake up in the morning and realize that God has given us another opportunity to share Jesus with others. We need to know that we are just passing through this world. God is more concerned with the faith of the believer than with the wrong doing of a sinner. Wrong doing does not hinder God; it takes the person deeper into the darkness of hell. But, the believer's lack of faith does not please God. Notice that if they had taken this man into the synagogue, they would have cast them out. If they would have taken this man to the Pharisees and Scribes, he would have died crippled. It was his friends who brought him to Jesus, and it is Jesus who wants us to bring others to Him. It could take a whole group to bring one person to Jesus. But there is nothing more exciting than friends who share their faith together.

Third, God gets excited when we forgive others their trespasses. When Jesus saw the faith of the men, Jesus said to the paralyzed man, "Your sins are forgiven." The Scribes were reasoning in their hearts, "Why doth this man thus speak blasphemies? who can forgive sins but God only?" And immediately when Jesus perceived in his spirit that they so reasoned within themselves, he said unto them, Why reason ye these things in your hearts? Whether is it easier to say to the sick of the palsy, Thy sins be forgiven thee; or to say, Arise, and take up thy bed, and walk? But that ye may know that the Son of man hath power on earth to forgive sins, (he saith to the sick of the palsy,) I say unto thee, Arise, and take up thy bed, and go thy way into thine house." (Mark 2:7-11) He just didn't heal this man. He converted, healed, and saved him! Praise God!

This is the way we should walk out of church; sanctified, clean, and washed by the Word of God and the Holy Spirit. (Ephesians 5:26) I want you to see two things in this story: the greatest thing people can do and the amazing thing God can do for us. The greatest thing we can do is to bring someone to Jesus. The amazing thing God can do for us is to say, "Your sins are forgiven." There are people who do not want to forgive.

There were two men, Jim Baker and Billy Graham, who over their lifetimes, had probably been admired by many people. Jim Baker landed in prison and received anger and bitterness from a public whose trust he had betrayed. Billy Graham went to visit him and extended a hand shake and a hug. He forgave him and extended the grace which he himself had enjoyed.

This is the Christian way of handling things. We all can enjoy this grace and forgiveness when we accept Jesus Christ into our hearts and live for Him. Now, this excites God when we seek forgiveness. People get saved and we testify to it and they confess it. This is something we can all do together, church! But, let me ask you "Are you excited about Jesus?" Then, let's stand and sing together our closing hymn, "Living for Jesus". Amen!

Worship Planning Helps #11

"Being confident of this very thing, that he which hath begun a good work in you will perform it until the day of Jesus Christ."
– Philippians 1:6

WELCOME:

Welcome to the house of the Lord! We gather, today, to worship and to remember that God is the author of new beginnings and the finisher of our faith. Let us worship Him!

INVOCATION:

God of grace and God of mercy,

Allow us to approach You even though our lives are marked by failure. Open before us the way that leads to life as You would have us live it. Meet with us, today, and teach us to live in Your grace and mercy and to make life a gracious place for those around us to live. In Jesus' name, we pray. Amen.

OFFERING PRAYER:

Eternal God,

Your grace blooms within us through the blessings of Your provisions. We bring to You our tithes and offerings. Bless those who are in need and use these gifts to fertilize the wilderness that the world might grow in Your ways. Amen.

PRAYER FOR THE FAMILY OF GOD:

Dear Heavenly Father,

We come to Thee, today, as a community of faith seeking Your guidance. Teach us to follow Your ways that we may be a good example to others. Furnish the material we need to grow spiritually that we may live a happy life, here in this world.

I pray for the congregation, O Lord. Bless them and send Your Holy Spirit to them that they may be filled with Your fruits and gifts. Bless them and their families. Take care of them, watch over them, and watch over their loved ones whom they care for. We unite with them, touching their petitions. We want to see Your glory and wondrous works in their lives. Lord, we use Your Word which is our promises.

We pray for the sick to recover. As Jesus said, "Rise and walk. Rise and be healed." You said there is healing in the house, today, Lord.

Bless and strengthen the brethren, Lord. Bless this church and prosper it. Bless those who come in and those who go out. Bless Your precious Word, today, and those who hear it. Strengthen them for new growth and new beginnings that they may conquer the things that need to be conquered and accomplish the things that will bring success in their lives. And to Your name be all the glory and the honor and the power forever. Amen.

BENEDICTION:
May the mercy and grace of our Lord be with you and with His Spirit teach you that God is working through you for goodness and righteousness.

SUGGESTED HYMNS:
"Amazing Grace"
"Softly and Tenderly"
"Heavenly Father, We Appreciate You"
"Thy Loving Kindness"
"Grace Greater Than Our Sin"

Sermon #11:
"Mercy and Grace"

Isaiah 63:7-9; Hebrews 4:12-16

It's a new year and the best way to begin this year is with mercy and grace and thanking the Lord for bringing us safely to it.

The Romans had a name and a meaning for everything, even their calendar. This is where we got our monthly names for our calendar. They were translated from the Roman calendar to our English calendar. February was named Februa, a time for a festival feast. Some months were named after the false gods the Romans worshipped. March was named after Mars, the god of war. May was named from the goddess, Maia. June was named after the goddess Juno. July was named in honor of Julius Caesar. August was named in honor of Caesar's descendant, Caesar Augustus. The next four months, September, October, November, and December were named after the Latin numbers in the Latin language. September was seven, and in Latin, was called septimbo. October was eight, and in Latin, was called octobio. November was nine, and in Latin, was called novena. December was ten, and in Latin, was called diesimbo. This was the order in which those months fell in the Roman calendar. The first month in the ancient Roman calendar was January, and this one had a descriptive name. Historians say that January comes from the god, Januas, a common god among the Romans. This god was a statue which had two faces, facing in two directions. The Latin word Janua means a door or window from which a person may look both ways, inward and outward, forward and backwards. And as we stand in the beginning of the month of January and a new year, we look back over the way we came through and we, also, look ahead to the new year where we are headed. As we celebrate this new year, we look at the year that has passed by with appreciation and we look at the year that lies ahead with anticipation. May we share this new year with the Word of God and also be moved to see God's mercy and grace in a new way.

In our scripture from Isaiah 63:7-9, Isaiah prophesied the changes the Messiah would bring to His people. He spoke about how he would preach to Israel, to those who were faithful to God. And then, Isaiah introduces his final portion of the prophecy with a prayer that recognizes all that the Lord did for His people; the kindness of the Lord, His compassion, and the deeds for which He is to be praised.

God said, "Surely they are my people." So, He became their Savior. In all their distress, He, too, was distressed, and the angel of His presence saved them. In His love and mercy, He redeemed them; He lifted them up and carried them all their days. We can see the loving kindness in God, and today, I will share about His loving kindness and the wonders for which He is to be praised.

We don't have to look too far back in the year to be reminded of God's undeserved love. In fact, we really only have to look back one week to Christmas. We were reminded that Jesus was born to live the holy life we have not lived and to die under the just punishment for our sins. This is mercy and grace; the kindness and love for us. We rejoice that we have had the privilege to celebrate his birthday and His great love for us. For fifty-two Sundays, God has fed us with His Word when we gathered for worship. We followed Jesus to the cross. We shouted, "He is alive!" We listened to His words and we have seen His mighty power. It is in God's Word that we have found healing and hope. We have felt God's presence and have been reassured of His love when we were troubled. And we called upon Him in faith as Psalm 50:15 instructs us to do. "And call upon me in the day of trouble: I will deliver thee, and thou shalt glorify me."

As we experience God's mercy and grace, we look back in appreciation. Isaiah acknowledged that the Lord had done many good things for His people. The Lord had brought His people out of slavery in Egypt. He fed them. He defeated their enemies. Through mighty miracles, He protected His people and prospered them. He blessed their crops and their other sources of income. This reminds us of what God did for His people in the Old Testament. And this is what God does for His people, today. Take a moment and look back in appreciation for all that the Lord has done in the past year. Who cannot tell of the deeds for which God is to be praised?

Some people might say, "I had problems and troubles. In fact, last year was one of the worst I have ever had. I lost my job. I was sick." We do face temptations, feel that way, and have those kinds of thoughts. And when Isaiah prayed this prayer, he was experiencing these same things. The people were going through persecution. Their nation was under the threat of foreign invasion. Things were bad and seemed very unclear. Yet, Isaiah knew that no matter how bad things were, God was with them. Isaiah knew that he was only seeing things from a human perspective. But, when he looked at things from the spiritual perspective, he knew God was concerned about them. Because of God's mercy, we can look back with appreciation, and because of Jesus' grace, we can move forward with anticipation. We are reminded that even when things looked bad, God was with us. It could have been worse. In verse 9, it says, "In all their affliction he was afflicted." God cares for us. Through all the trials and troubles we faced, last year, God was merciful to us. It always makes us feel better when someone knows what we are going through. That is a reason to celebrate God's mercy and Jesus' grace. Verse 9 continues, "and the angel of his presence saved them." We may never know how many disasters the Lord protected us from. We may have walked through the valley of the shadow of death and not even realized it. But, we do know the Lord's presence saved us. Prophetically, this verse is referring to Jesus Christ. Verse 9 concludes, "In his love and in his pity he redeemed them; and he bare them, and carried them all the days of old." Through everything, Jesus was there. As we celebrate Jesus' grace, we look back with appreciation for God's protection. The Lord said through Isaiah in chapter forty-six, verses three and four, "Hearken unto me, O house of Jacob, and all the remnant of the house of Israel, which are borne by me from the belly, which are carried from the womb: And even to your old age I am he; and even to hoar hairs will I carry you: I have made, and I will bear; even I will carry, and will deliver you." From our youth to our old age, God promises to be with us. From year to year, God will sustain us. As we look back at another year of God's protection, may we trust in God. He used all the things that seem bad to draw us into a closer relationship with Him.

When a baby giraffe is born, his mother does something that we might consider cruel. The mother gives her baby a kick. When he doesn't get up, the mother gives it another kick. This process is repeated until the baby giraffe slowly stands up. Then, the mother knocks the baby giraffe down, again, so he remembers how he got up. Why does the mother do this? The baby giraffe has to be able to walk very quickly after birth. There are lions, hyenas, and leopards that enjoy baby giraffes. If the mother didn't do what looks like a cruel thing, the baby would never survive. The Lord does a similar thing to us through our trials and frustrations. He permits us to stumble to teach us a lesson.

There was a pastor of a church who announced that it was time for children's Sunday school. One little girl stood up and said, "Let's go, Lord, and ran to her Sunday school room. On the corner of the hallway, as she turned, she slipped and fell. Getting up, she said, "Okay, Lord, let's try, again. But this time, don't push me, okay?"

In II Corinthians 4, Paul teaches us how to be strong and face the attacks of the devil with God's Word. Our struggles have made us stronger. We have learned to rely on God more faithfully. God has been with us.

The other part of our New Year's celebration is looking ahead. We make resolutions. But, we also know that our God's mercy is renewed every day. For another year, we will build up our faith and seek guidance for our lives. Instead of looking ahead to the New Year with fear, let us hear these words from the Lord. "In all their affliction he was afflicted, and the angel of his presence saved them: in his love and in his pity he redeemed them; and he bare them, and carried them all the days of old." In any distress that might come our way, God will be with us. He will rescue us and carry us through even the worst of times.

So, how does our knowledge of God's mercy and grace for this New Year affect us? In good times and in the bad times, God is always with us. That truth allows me to stand before you, this morning, and preach with confidence.

A farmer had some puppies he needed to sell. He painted a sign advertising the pups and set about nailing it to a post on the edge of his yard. As he was pounding the last nail into the post, he felt a tug on his overalls. He looked down at a little boy. "Hey, Mister, I want to buy one of your puppies." "Well," said the farmer as he rubbed the sweat off his neck, "these puppies come from fine parents and cost a lot of money." The boy dropped his head for a moment. Then, he reached into his pocket and pulled out a handful of change and held it up to the farmer. "I've got thirty nine cents. Is that enough to take a look?" "Sure," said the farmer. And with that, the farmer let out a whistle, "Here, Dolly!" Out from the dog house and down the ramp ran Dolly followed by four little puppies. The little boy pressed his face against the chain link fence. His eyes danced with delight. As the dogs made their way to the fence, the little boy noticed something else stirring inside the dog house. Slowly, another little puppy (smaller than the rest) slid down the ramp. Then, in an awkward manner, the little pup began hobbling toward the others, doing its best to catch up. "I want that one!" The little boy said, pointing to the weakest. The farmer knelt down at the boy's side and said, "Son, you don't want that puppy. He will never be able to run and play with you like these other puppies." With that, the little boy stepped back from the fence, reached down, and began rolling up one leg of his pants. In doing so, he revealed a steel brace running down both sides of his leg attaching itself to a specially made shoe. Looking back up at the farmer, he said, "You see, sir, I don't run too well myself, either, and he will need someone who understands him."

God knows what you may be going through and remember He is the One who created you. God loves you and thinks of you often. Never let anyone tell you that God does not care about you or love you. In the past year, we have enjoyed His love and grace and blessings. He has felt our pain and sorrow. He has provided us with what we needed, both physically and spiritually, and has comforted us. Today, in this New Year, celebrate God's grace; grace that will pardon and cleanse within, grace that is greater than all our sin. Amen.

Worship Planning Helps #12

"But ye shall receive power, after that the Holy Ghost is come upon you."
- Acts 1:8

WELCOME:

Today is the Sunday when we celebrate the Holy Spirit giving life to the church. The first Christians became a family of one heart and soul. We, too, can be in union with one another if we allow the Holy Spirit to fill our hearts. We extend a warm welcome to all.

INVOCATION:

Spirit of God, quiet our hearts, heal our anxious thoughts, free us from our fretful ways. Breathe on us Your holy calm so that in the stillness of Your presence, we may open ourselves to trust and be transformed. Amen.

OFFERING PRAYER:

Through Your Spirit, O God, You give Yourself to us. Now, through these tithes and offerings, we give ourselves to You. Use them to teach the world of Your love for them. Amen.

PRAYER FOR THE FAMILY OF GOD:

Thank You, Gracious God, for revealing Yourself to us in Jesus Christ. Through Jesus, we can see how much You love us. Through Jesus, we hear Your teachings of love and mercy. Through the Holy Spirit, we can feel the joy to which You call us. Through the Spirit, we can know that You are light; and we want to walk in the light. Come into the shadowy places of our lives and our world with Your light. Illumine our hearts and minds to do Your will and walk in Your ways. Bring those who are living without light and hope to us that we may show them Your love. I pray for our church congregation, O Lord. Open their minds that they may have a deeper understanding in Your Word and in Your gifts that You want to bless them with the power of Your Holy Spirit. Amen.

BENEDICTION:

Go in the power of the Holy Spirit who knows your every need, who prays for you, and who gives you energy to do God's will, this coming week, in His name. Amen!

SUGGESTED HYMNS:

"Showers of Blessing"
"Heavenly Father, We Appreciate You"

"Turn Your Eyes Upon Jesus"
"Holy, Holy"
"Lord, Listen to Your Children Praying"
"Spirit of the Living God"

Sermon #12:
"There's Power in the Church"

Acts 2:1-4

Wouldn't it be wonderful if we didn't have to go through all the suffering and pain and spiritual battles? Just to show up here on church days and experience the power of God in our lives? Just to have the power to overcome temptation, the power to live in purity, and the power to share Jesus with our friends? Just walk into the church and walk out with a blessing to live a life for Jesus Christ? But to have that kind of power requires showing up on church days and making up our minds to have that kind of power. But to have that kind of power will require preparation. This is how we find the disciples of Jesus in the upper room. They were waiting for the power of God to fall upon their lives. You probably know what happened in Acts 2.

After the Holy Spirit came upon these followers of Jesus, they experienced a great spiritual growth. They also had a great number in growth as thousands repented of their sin and turned to Jesus, believed, and accepted Him as their Lord and Savior. What an incredible movement of God! How we long to see that kind of power in us and among us! But, not without preparation!

We will never experience Acts 2 without first experiencing Acts 1. "But ye shall receive power, after that the Holy Ghost is come upon you: and ye shall be witnesses unto me both in Jerusalem, and in all Judaea, and in Samaria, and unto the uttermost part of the earth." First comes preparation and then comes power. And last, but not least, we discover in Acts 1, that the apostles' preparation included the authority of scripture.

We have to get our lives back under the authority of the Word. We can't have rebellion against God's Word although there will be refusal to live under its authority and there will be the absence of God's Spirit. That is true in everybody's life, everybody's marriage, and everybody's church. The way to prepare for God's power to fall upon our lives begins with the authority of the Word of God in our Christian life. This is very important. Paul says, in Hebrews 4:12, "For the word of God is quick, and powerful, and sharper than any two-edged sword, piercing even to the dividing asunder of soul and spirit, and of the joints and marrow, and is a discerner of the thoughts and intents of the heart."

The disciples of Jesus made prayer a priority. They fought and fussed much of the time, but it wasn't until they prayed themselves into one accord, that the power of God fell upon them.

We learn in the book of Acts that God's power doesn't fall upon a divided fellowship. Paul says, in Ephesians 4:3, "Endeavoring to keep the unity of the Spirit in the bond of peace." To strive means to make an effort to achieve something. In Romans 14:19, Paul says, "Let us therefore follow after the things which make for peace, and things wherewith one may edify another." It wasn't until they followed these words that the power of God fell upon them. As they prayed, God began to change their hearts and their personal agendas were released. Their desires and positions, their pride and egos were vanished, and as they came together in unity, God set His power upon them and the church exploded with growth; both physical and spiritual. Can you see it? We need to strive to be in church. Getting back to the basics means that every member is working together, promoting the unity of our church.

In Proverbs 6:19, Solomon knew that seven deadly sins were creeping into the people. Then, they were bringing them into the church; the house of God. And because of this, people were getting sick and dying and rejecting their fellowship. God hates sin; and some of them are lies, false witnesses, sowing division among the children of God. Sowing discord keeps the power of God away from us. Stay away from false statements; they will harm us. We read in I Corinthians 12:20, "But now are they many members, yet but one body." And in I Corinthians 10:24, we read, "Let no man seek his own, but every man another's wealth." It is not what is good for me, but what is good for you! There is power in unity. We are putting the Word of God into practice.

David says, in Psalm 133:1 & 2, "Behold, how good and how pleasant it is for brethren to dwell together in unity! It is like the precious ointment upon the head, that ran down upon the beard, even Aaron's beard: that went down to the skirts of his garments;." It is a promise commanded by the Lord for life eternal. God has blessed us with over three thousand, seven hundred promises in His Word. This is what we find taking place in Acts 1; unity and preparation. Now, that they were prepared for the power from God; the power would change their lives, their families, their fellowship, their communities, their towns, and eventually, the whole world. So, let's see what happens and how it happened and what it means for us, today, as we get back to the basics.

Let's begin reading in Acts 2:1-4. "And when the day of Pentecost was fully come, they were all with one accord in one place. And suddenly there came a sound from heaven as of a rushing mighty wind, and it filled all the house where they were sitting. And there appeared unto them cloven tongues like as of fire, and it sat upon each of them. And they were all filled with the Holy Ghost, and began to speak with other tongues, as the Spirit gave them utterance." Now, Jesus had told them this would happen. He told them, in Acts 1:8, "But ye shall receive power, after that the Holy Ghost is come upon you: and ye shall be witnesses unto me both in Jerusalem, and in all Judaea, and in Samaria, and unto the uttermost part of the earth." He deliberately chose Pentecost to send down His power!

Now, what is Pentecost, anyway? Well, Pentecost was the Jewish harvest festival when they would come before God with their offerings and thanksgiving for the harvest. It was something like our Thanksgiving Day we celebrate every year. The word Pentecost means fiftieth day. They started counting at the Passover, which commemorated their exodus from Egypt, and counted off forty nine days. The fiftieth day was Pentecost! They had been celebrating Pentecost since the days of Moses.

Now, let's see what happened. The church became empowered which means there is power in the church because the church is nothing more than the sum total of the membership. Acts 2:1 says, "And when the day of Pentecost was fully come, they were all with one accord in one place." Can you imagine forty nine days in one place, worshipping and praising God, sleeping and eating in the coffee house? Now, let me mention here that when we read that they were with one accord in one place, the Greek says they were all joined together. In Acts 1:14, they were all in one purpose and in one mind. They prayed themselves into one accord. In Matthew 18:19, 20, Jesus said, "Again I say unto you, That if two of you shall agree on earth as touching any thing that they shall ask, it shall be done for them of my Father which is in heaven. For where two or three are gathered together in my name, there am I in the midst of them." Now, they not only had union, but they had unity. What's the difference between union and unity? Well, if you take two cats and tie their tails together, they will be in union. But, they are not going to be in unity!

Now, as the church became stronger, I want you to notice in Acts 2:2 how it all happened. "And suddenly there came a sound from heaven as of a rushing mighty wind, and it filled all the house where they were sitting." Right there, where they were sitting, without any warning, something happened; a sound in their ears. Luke says that this sound was as of a rushing mighty wind. This was the only way they could describe it. This started their celebration and all the commotion. That wind was a symbol of the Holy Spirit. You might say, 'But, I don't understand it." Well, in John 3:8, Jesus says, "The wind bloweth where it listeth, and thou hearest the sound thereof, but canst not tell whence it cometh, and whither it goeth: so is every one that is born of the Spirit." Like the wind, it gives us a chill in our bodies.

The Holy Spirit of God is the third person of the Trinity. It might not be visible to the physical eye, but it is visible to the spiritual eye; and you can even see His impact. Jesus states that the Holy Spirit will feel like a wind passing through your body. That's the Holy Spirit of God! You will feel a chill coming across your body when you are worshipping Jesus or sharing or evangelizing or witnessing. That's the Holy Spirit working to convict the person of sin and convince the person of the truth of the Word of God. It is "the Spirit itself [who] beareth witness with our spirit, that we are the children of God." (Romans 8:16) It is the Holy Spirit that leads and guides us. Thank God every time you feel this chill which is the Holy Spirit! This is what God wants you to do from now on.

Luke says that the sound filled everybody. You talk about having surrounding feelings of the Spirit; they had it and it was experienced by one hundred twenty of them. Everybody in the city heard them celebrating, and came to see what was happening. Now, how would you like to hear testimonies about something like that? We can, by sharing our testimonies and letting the Holy Spirit fall afresh on us, to melt us and to mold us, to fill us and to use us. So, when we are feeling weak, let the Spirit of the living God fall afresh on us. Amen, church? Amen!

Worship Planning Helps #13

"And when you believed in Christ, He identified you as His own
by giving you the Holy Spirit, whom He promised long ago."
- Ephesians 1:13

WELCOME:

On this first Sunday of the New Year, it is a privilege to worship the Lord and get our lives in tune with the will of God. We welcome all who have come. Let us begin the New Year with Christian love for one another.

INVOCATION:

Almighty God, we are Your people, and through Jesus Christ, You have made us Your children. May our love for You be poured out in praise and worship to You. In this time of worship, we give You thanks for Your many blessings. We pray that Your Holy Spirit will give us new strength and courage to share the Good News of Jesus with others. Amen.

OFFERING PRAYER:

Dear God,

You give us life. You send us to do Your work in this world. You call us to bring our tithes and offerings to You to use as You see fit. Help us listen and hear Your call, and to respond with gladness to do Your will, every day of our lives. We offer ourselves for Your service. In Jesus' name, Amen.

PRAYER FOR THE FAMILY OF GOD:

Loving God,

We lay our heads upon Your shoulder and rest in comfort. We know You created us out of great love to receive and share Your blessings. As Your chosen ones, help us remember the glory in which we were created. Where there is ugliness, help us create beauty. Where there is desolation, help us produce bounty. Help us show others they are precious to us as You have shown us we are precious to You. Teach us, Lord, to glorify You and all of Your creation. Magnify Yourself in us that we may truly honor You. Let Your precious Word be verified among Your people and Your glory be manifested among all people. We exalt You above all gods. Let Your Spirit speak to us.

I pray for those who are sick, confused, hurting, and lost, today. Bring them before Your mighty presence of holiness and touch their needs. Cause them to lift up their eyes to You and to find You to be their source of all healing, quiet assurance, and guidance. Bless them, today, that they might be Your instruments in this world. In Jesus' name, Amen.

BENEDICTION:

We aren't the same anymore. God is making us like His Son. May the world see the family resemblance in us. We go into the world as children of God, redeemed by His Son. Go out to serve and do God's will. Amen.

SUGGESTED HYMNS:

"To God Be the Glory"
"Praise Him! Praise Him!"
"He Touched Me"
"Something Beautiful"
"I Love to Tell the Story"
"Blessed Assurance"

Sermon #13:
"The Beginning of a New Year"

John 1:12-18 & Ephesians 1:1-14

Christmas has come and gone. For some people, they wish it was longer, and for some, they are still sighing in relief! Whew! I'm glad it is over! Some of us are here, looking to find a little peace and quiet at the end of the storm. Some of us are here, because if we were home, we would be cleaning up and putting away Christmas boxes. But, did Christmas really meet all of our expectations?

It is the first Sunday in a New Year, and this is the best way to start: in church, worshiping our Lord and Savior, Jesus Christ! Wouldn't it be nice if we could begin a New Year with a new life and a new Master like the Lord Jesus Christ?

There is a true story about a woman who attended every service of the church. She was blind and needed to take her guide dog along with her. The dog would enter with the lady and sit quietly beside her during the whole service. The lady always sat on an outside seat by the aisle. At the conclusion of the service, the woman would always go and kneel at the altar for prayer, and the dog would always sit faithfully by her side, as the lady prayed for her husband to give his life to the Lord Jesus. The woman's husband was a cruel man who deeply resented her devotion to Jesus Christ. He would make fun of her for going to church. But, one day, she felt sick and went to see her doctor who admitted her to the hospital for further tests. However, before the tests were completed, she passed on to heaven. After the woman's funeral, only the man and the dog were left at home. But, the man noticed something unusual. The dog disappeared, every Wednesday evening at 7:00 p.m., and didn't return home for two hours. Every Sunday morning, the dog would disappear, too. Then, he would reappear two hours later. One Sunday, the man decided to follow the dog and see where he went. Hurrying to keep up with the dog, the man followed the dog to that little church where his wife had attended so faithfully and prayed for his salvation. He watched as the dog took its seat on the aisle while the service went on. At the end of the service, the dog got up and went up front to the altar and took his place where the man's wife would kneel and pray for her husband. The man was so touched that he went forward and knelt down, right next to the dog, where his wife would kneel. He repented and answered the Lord's call. From then on, the dog found a new master.

Paul says, in Hebrews 11:6, "But without faith it is impossible to please him: for he that cometh to God must believe that he is, and that he is a rewarder of them that diligently seek him."

The truth is, that along with the layout of emotions tied to this season, many are feeling a little bit down. Deep inside, there is a sense of disappointment. It is as if somewhere, in all of the going and giving and getting and blessing, we missed something; and we just don't know how to respond to it. That's how it was for Mary and Joseph. They were running for their lives because of Herod the King. They had been warned and guided by Gabriel, God's angel, to flee for their safety. They found that safety in God.

In Luke 2:25-35, we find a man named Simeon. He was a just and devout man who was waiting for the consolation of Israel. The Holy Spirit spoke to him and directed him to go to the temple for the dedication of Jesus. Simeon didn't know Mary and Joseph were coming to Jerusalem with Jesus. But, it was the Holy Spirit who told him. He found satisfaction in meeting Jesus!

In Luke 2:36-38, we read of Anna, a devout church lady. She would not miss an assembly in the church at all. She was a fasting and praying, eighty-four year old believer. She had been married for seven years, when she was young, and had remained a widow ever since. She heard the good news and started witnessing about the baby Jesus to all the people who were looking forward to the redemption of Jerusalem. She found joy in proclaiming Jesus!

To Simeon and Anna, it was the Holy Spirit who rewarded them. But, are we any different? No, we are all instruments of God. God is using us and we all have a desire to grow stronger in the Spirit and to see the gifts of the Holy Spirit manifested in our lives. We are blessed that we are not like those who are outside of the covenant. In II Corinthians 3:2, Paul says, "Ye are our epistle written in our hearts, known and read of all men:" We lean wholly and completely on Jesus Christ, our Lord, because we love to come to church and worship our oneness with Jesus Christ. You do love to worship, don't you? It is our time of freedom, our time of thanksgiving, and our time of celebration. This house is our filling station. We come here to fill up in order to face another day, another week, and another year.

But, let me ask you. Have you ever been persecuted for righteousness or laughed at for your trials and tribulations? Have they ever mocked you behind your back because they are convinced that you are just pretending to be strong? Do they make fun of you while they go to happy hour? Do they laugh when you go to church and they stay home to watch the game? Do they make fun of you because you choose to pay tithes rather than buying an expensive car like the one they drive? If they do laugh, it is because they don't understand that our soul is our most valuable possession. If it had not been for Jesus we would be lost like they are. They just don't understand that worshiping Jesus is not an option. It is an obligation and a requirement! It is our happy hour; a product of our grateful hearts. They don't understand that our tithe is our investment for our future. They don't understand that it is the beginning of a New Year, and this is the best way to start it.

I wish there was an easier way to make our friends and loved ones see how much God loves them; some magic word that would open their eyes, their minds, and their hearts and cause them to drop instantly to their knees. But, it is their decision with the Lord. We are just planting seeds and God is reaping the harvest. So, today's scripture answers the tough questions that most often are asked when we share our faith and God's plan of salvation with others. The Living Bible is an easier translation to read to someone who hasn't heard the Word of God. In Romans 10:9 & 10, Paul says, "That if thou shalt confess with thy mouth the Lord Jesus, and shalt believe in thine heart that God hath raised him from the dead, thou shalt be saved. For with the heart man believeth unto righteousness; and with the mouth confession is made unto salvation." Everyone must be saved through their own personal confession. When someone asks, "What must I do to be saved?" or "Why do I even need God, anyway?", we simply point them to Jesus. Remember, we can't convince a person to accept Jesus unless they are ready for God. People's attitudes are self-centered. They think, "What can God give me that I can't give myself? What do I need God for?" Well, if someone is drowning, you can't throw him a lesson book on how to swim! But, you can throw him a lifeline! And, if he grabs it, then reel him in to the book of Romans and the road of salvation or take him to John's way to salvation where Jesus is explaining to Nicodemus the way to be born, again.

But, how do you make someone see that he or she needs salvation? You have to paint the picture, first, of what God has to offer. We can share our testimony, telling how we answered the Lord's call, and how salvation and strength came to us, at that moment, and how the kingdom of God and the power of Jesus Christ are ours. Tell them how "the accuser of our brethren is cast down, which accused them before our God day and night. And [how you] overcame him by the blood of the Lamb, and by the word of [your] testimony." (Revelation 12:10-11) That's what God has done for us and how we have surrendered our devotion and our will to the purpose of God, one hundred percent! Jesus prayed in the Garden of Gethsemane, "Not as I will, but as thou wilt." (Matthew 26:39)

Now, from the looks of the world, most sinners would rather risk dying than repent and be baptized into God's family. They would rather wear a sign around their necks stating, "Why do I need God?" The answer is plain and simple, "Without God, you will die in sin. And nobody wants to die." It won't be because God rejected them. It will be because they rejected God. That is why it is so urgent for us to witness to the lost. His presence within us is God's guarantee that He will give us all that He promises us. The Spirit's seal upon us means that God has already purchased us and that He guarantees to bring us to Himself. This is just one of the reasons we serve our glorious God.

This is the beginning of a New Year. In church, we can praise Him for His tender mercies and for His guidance and protection, every day. We can praise Him for His provision of food and shelter. We can praise Him for the love of our family and friends and for the abundant life

He grants us. We can praise Him for the wisdom He imparts and for the strength He gives us to resist temptation. We can praise Him for the opportunity to serve in His kingdom and for the joy that He restores in us. And when our service is done, here, we will have a seat in heaven with Him. When we leave this world of despair, we will be caught up to meet Him in the air, already judged and all dressed up!

This is why we submit to God's authority. That's why we are faithful to God. That's why we are obedient to God's commandments. This is why we fellowship with God's people and commit to God's cause. Because we are faithful, dedicated, committed, born again, new creations, children of God, the called and the chosen, we can trust God's judgment and rejoice in God's glory and in His word! "Well done, thou good and faithful servant: thou hast been faithful over a few things, I will make thee ruler over many things: enter thou into the joy of thy lord." (Matthew 25:36)

If you are not sure of this, I extend His invitation. "That if thou shalt confess with thy mouth the Lord Jesus, and shalt believe in thine heart that God hath raised him from the dead, thou shalt be saved. For with the heart man believeth unto righteousness; and with the mouth confession is made unto salvation." (Romans 10:9-10) I pray you have made your decision. If not, I hope you will do so as we sing our closing song.

Worship Planning Helps #14

*"Blessed be the King that cometh in the name of the
Lord: peace in heaven, and glory in the highest."*
– Luke19:38

WELCOME:

Welcome to this Palm Sunday service. The crowds in Jerusalem welcomed the humble arrival of the King with palms and shouts of "Hosanna!" Let us honor and praise Him, today, with that same joyful spirit.

INVOCATION:

God of Passion and Palms,

Come to us, this day. Enter into our hearts as You once entered into Jerusalem, full of passion and purpose. Help us to receive You with joy and thanksgiving. Fill us with the mind of Christ that we may be Your disciples on this earth. May we live our lives with Your passion and purpose that we might proclaim Your name wherever You lead us to go. In Jesus' name, Amen.

OFFERING PRAYER:

We bring these gifts to You, O Lord, not because you need them, but because we need to bring them. They are reminders of Your bountiful grace and matchless love. We offer them to You with thanksgiving. Amen.

PRAYER FOR THE FAMILY OF GOD:

In Jesus' name, we come to You, Father. When we are together, we are a needy bunch, O Lord; confused, easily distracted, fearful, and often in pain. We bring to You such a wounded mass of humanity, wondering if You can do anything with us. Bind up our wounds. Settle our confusion and help us to focus on You and what You want. Keep us away from false hope and move us toward true hope. Forgive us for our sin. Help us to grow stronger and more determined to stay in one accord. Heal the pain we impose on ourselves, as well as the pain that comes to us simply because we are human. Help us to remember the way You are leading us is the way, the truth, and the life. Bless the petitions of the congregation, this morning, with a touch from Your healing hand. Thank You, Lord, in Jesus' name, Amen.

BENEDICTION:

Go forth into the world to proclaim with joy that Jesus is able to heal the wounded and breathe new hope into the discouraged. Go forth and live in the hope and joy that Jesus came to give

His people. Go and rejoice as you remember "blessed is He who comes in the name of the Lord." Amen.

SUGGESTED HYMNS:
"Praise Him! Praise Him!"
"Blessed Be the Name"
"He is Lord"
"His Name is Wonderful"
"There is a Balm in Gilead"
"Alleluia"

Sermon #14:
"Jesus Wept on Palm Sunday"

Luke 19:28-41

The Sunday school teacher looked at the class of four year olds and asked, "Does anyone know what today is?" A little girl waved her hand, "I know! I know! Today is Palm Sunday." "Right," the teacher replied. "Does anyone know what next Sunday is?" The same little girl held up her hand, "I know! I know! Next Sunday is Easter Sunday!" Then, the teacher asked, "Does anyone know what makes next Sunday Easter?" The little girl responded, "Yes, next Sunday is Easter Sunday because Jesus rose from the grave. And, if He sees His shadow, He has to go back into His grave for six more weeks." She almost had it right.

Palm Sunday is a day of celebration and victory for the Christian church. Some young Christians don't know the story of Jesus riding victoriously into Jerusalem. Many of the people who participated in the Passover were worshiping Jesus. Even the disciples got caught up in that moment of praising, saying, "Blessed is he that cometh in the name of the Lord; Hosanna in the highest." (Matthew 21:9) In Matthew 23:39, Jesus says, "For I say unto you, Ye shall not see me henceforth, till ye shall say, Blessed is he that cometh in the name of the Lord."

The crowd reverently threw palm branches and garments on the ground as a sign of victory and many of them called him king, at least for a while. We read in Luke 19:41, "And when he was come near, he beheld the city [Jerusalem], and wept over it." While the people were yelling hosanna which means "Save, I pray thee," Jesus wept. (John 11:35) This is the smallest scripture in the Bible. Luke says that Jesus saw the city in its beautiful, breath taking view. He saw the display and the parade of the Passover celebration. He saw the splendor of the two million Jews pressing through the city gates. And He wept.

What was the cause that made Jesus weep? It was the spiritual poverty of His Father's chosen people. He wept for their little faith. He wept for the lost prodigal son and daughter in the city. He wept for the people who were in sin and the pain that people were going through. He wept because the people weren't ready for His visitation. He wept because people did not know who He was or who He belonged to. He wept because people did not realize that He was the One whom Zechariah prophesied saying, "Rejoice greatly, O daughter of Zion; shout, O daughter of Jerusalem: behold, thy King cometh unto thee: he is just, and having salvation; lowly, and riding upon [a donkey], and upon a colt the foal of [a donkey]." (Zechariah 9:9) Jesus wept because He cared.

And He still does! He cares for you in the same way He cared for the assembly of the Passover celebrants on that day. He cares about your sin and your pain. He cares, every time, Christians go astray. He cares because He loves us and He weeps. He weeps because He knows how wonderful life could be, if only you gave your heart over to Him instead of your wondering mind. He weeps because He knows your full potential.

But, the question is: Is Jesus weeping on this Palm Sunday for you? Are you as excited about Jesus as He is about you? Are you right with Jesus and with God? Christ is not looking at what we are. He is looking at what we can become with His help. Sure, we can go through life without Him. But, we will always miss the mark without Him. We will always miss the goal He has in mind for us. His goal is for us to achieve emotionally, socially, and financially. His goal is for us to achieve spiritually, too. Jesus wants us to rise above the level of the average and become spiritually strong. He wants us to achieve things no worldly life can promise us. Jesus wants us to have salvation. (John 3:16) Jesus wants us to have eternal life. In John 11:25, Jesus says, "I am the resurrection, and the life: he that believeth in me, though he were dead, yet shall he live." Jesus wants us to have peace. Philippians 4:7 says, "And the peace of God, which passeth all understanding, shall keep your hearts and minds through Christ Jesus." He wants us to have strength. "I can do all things through Christ which strengtheneth me." (Philippians 4:13) Notice, that in all four of these scriptures, the promises of God - salvation, eternal life, peace, and strength - are only offered by Jesus Christ. Our belief in Jesus gives us salvation. Our belief in Him gives us eternal life. It gives us strength and peace.

People can try to live life to the fullest without Jesus, but they will fail; never knowing their rewards. These rewards might require a change of life. Maybe, some people don't want to be different. Maybe, some are unwilling to break away from the crowd. Well, here is what Jesus wants you to know. He knows your full potential. He knows the pathway you must take that leads to eternal joy.

But, you must break away from the crowd and follow Him. You have to be willing to accept Jesus' invitation to walk alone with Him. It is time to break away. You will never reach your full potential by your own charming influence. It is time to break away. You will never reach your full potential with your own efforts. You will never reach your full potential by your own careful judgment or your own quality of character or your own high standards or you own generous nature or your own natural talent or your own dedicated devotion. You cannot reach your full potential without Jesus Christ! We need to break away and follow Jesus.

He will wash away your sins. He will lift your soul and spirit from humiliation. He will clean you from corruption. He will set you free from the bondage of trusting only in yourself. He will lead you to your full potential in your walk with Jesus Christ. Because salvation comes from the work Jesus Christ did for us while rewards depend upon the work we do for Jesus.

Someone had a dream about Heaven's Grocery store. He said, "One day, I saw a sign that read *"Heaven's Grocery Store"*. As I got a little closer, the door opened wide and I found myself standing inside. I saw a host of angels. One handed me a basket and said, "My child, shop with care. Everything a human needs is in this store, and if you need some more, you can come tomorrow for more." First, I got some patience. Love was in the same row. Further down was understanding; you need that everywhere you go. I got two bags of wisdom and two bags of faith. I just couldn't miss the Holy Ghost for it was all over the place. I stopped to get some strength and courage to help me run the race. By then, my basket was getting full. But, I remembered I needed some grace. I didn't forget salvation for it was free. I got enough of that for you and me. Then, I went to the counter to pay my grocery bill; for I thought I had everything I needed to do my Master's will. As I went up the aisle, I saw prayer, and I just had to put that in. I knew when I stepped outside, I would run into sin. Peace and joy were plentiful; they were on the shelf. Song and praise were hanging near, so, I just helped myself. Then, I said to the angel, "Now, how much do I owe?" He smiled and said, "My child, Jesus paid your bill, a long, long time ago."

Palm Sunday is a day of celebration. The battle has been won! The King is here among us! All burdens will be lifted. All diseases will find their balm in Gilead. All loneliness will find a faithful companion. All darkness will dissolve in the presence of His radiance. Bring your burdens, diseases, loneliness, and darkness to Jesus. Come before Him! Our Savior is ready to turn His followers into sanctified saints. I hear Him saying, "Today is God's gift, a day made for us. Today is His day made for thanks. Today, we gather in joy and thanksgiving, in sorrow and grief, remembering Jesus' gift of great love." And I still hear Him saying, "I am Alpha and Omega, the beginning and the end, the first and the last." (Revelation 22:13) Amen!

Worship Planning Helps #15

"The great day of the Lord is near, it is near, and hasteth greatly, even the voice of the day of the Lord: the mighty man shall cry there bitterly."
– Zephaniah 1:14

WELCOME:
We extend a warm welcome to you in the name of our Lord and Savior, Jesus Christ As we worship, may we be drawn closer to God.

INVOCATION:
God of us all,
Grant to us, Your children, the wisdom to know that all we need and desire can be found in You. Keep us from seeking after the things of the world that do not satisfy. Let our hearts seek after You and our lives be committed to following after You.

OFFERING PRAYER:
We offer to You, O God, these tithes and offerings as symbols of our devotion to You. We look to You for the material needs of our lives, knowing that You alone are our Provider. Bless these gifts that others may know You and be ready to meet You when You return to take Your people home. Amen.

PRAYER FOR THE FAMILY OF GOD:
Dear Heavenly Father, in Jesus' name, we come to You. We worship You as the God of all creation, for You alone hold everything in Your hands. All things belong to You, including our lives, and we give You thanks for the blessings that You have bestowed upon us. We thank You for the abundance of creation and for all the things that make life easier for us. We thank You for Your Son, Jesus, who is worthy to bear Your precious holy name that You have revealed to us. Help us to use Your gifts wisely and to not allow them to become idols. Guide us to keep our eyes on You, the Giver, and not on the gifts that we might glorify Your name and strive to be ready for the day of Your soon coming. Amen.

BENEDICTION:
Go and spread the good news that all may know the fullness of life through Jesus Christ our Lord. Share the message that life is more than material things and proclaim with boldness the good news that Jesus Christ is coming soon. Amen.

SUGGESTED HYMNS:
"How Great Thou Art"
"The King Is Coming"
"I Need Thee Every Hour"
"When the Roll Is Called Up Yonder"
"Amazing Grace"

Sermon #15:
"The Mighty Day of the Lord"
Zephaniah 1 & Psalm 90

The book of Zephaniah is a small book that is three chapters long, and pastors seldom preach from it. I would say that not one person in one hundred has heard a sermon preached from Zephaniah. This little book of prophecy is one of the most forgotten scriptures in all of God's Word. It is not even found in the New Testament for references. Zephaniah is, perhaps, the least known book of the Old Testament, and yet, it has so much to offer.

This story unfolds between 625 and 610 B. C. Zephaniah means "Yahweh hides or protects". He was the great, great grandson of King Hezekiah; therefore, he was of royal blood. The prophet was related to Josiah. He ministered during the days of King Josiah who was Judah's last godly ruler. The scripture tells us, that in those days, King Josiah was the God-fearing son of Amon who, with his father Mannasseh, were two of the most wicked kings in Israel's history. (II Kings 2 & 3) These two evil kings had hidden God's commandments. Zephaniah's ministry helped to prepare for the great revival, in 621 B. C., which occurred under Josiah's reign, when the law of Moses was rediscovered during the repair of the temple. (II Chronicles 34 & 35)

Zephaniah, the prophet, pronounces judgment upon the land of God. The purpose of his message was to set forth what the day of the Lord would mean to the ungodly people of Judah and the godly remnant from Israel. The theme of this book is "The Day of the Lord" which destroys the false remainder of Baal and destroys the God-ignoring nation.

King Josiah ordered the people of Judah and Israel to stop sinning. The changes Josiah made in the people were sincere, on his part, but changed only a small portion of the people, and only in the form of religion. There was no real change of heart among the people. There was very little reformation without transformation. You could not give the people of Israel or Judah a message without the presence of the Lord because they knew the presence of Yahweh. We, too, not only need to know His word, but the presence of His Holy Spirit, also.

This was the time in which Zephaniah came to minister, and his message was clear. He spoke of the coming day of the Lord. This phrase, "the coming of the Lord," is a prophecy of the judgment in the Old Testament. God chose Zephaniah to declare the future punishment to a rebellious people. He set forth the words, "that great and terrible day of the Lord," and then, he spoke directly to Judah and Israel. This was the custom in those days; to put forth a proclamation, and then, share the message of the Lord. Zephaniah portrayed a picture of a miserable future. God would sweep away everything in the land and destroy it to the ground.

Judah had worshiped Baal, the great god of the Canaanite pantheon, and Milcom of the Ammonites; thus, ignoring the only true God, Yaweh. (Zephaniah 1:5) This period of time was as wicked as Sodom and Gomorrah. It is no wonder the name of the judgment was "the terrible day of the Lord."

I want to share three points on this prophecy.

First point: Do you know that the time is at hand? The phrase, "at hand," means quickly. God will make the time go by so fast for the sinner. The prophet had to wake up this nation from its impending danger. Warning them with the judgment pronounced on all the nations with "The Day of the Lord is at hand." They were so close to the judgment day and they didn't even know it. Where were the singers and the choir of the Lord? They believed the false accusations on the holy nation. We have to be careful not to accept the false accusations against the people of God. But did it work? No, the nation of Israel rejected the prophets of God and continued to sin and worship Baal, the same god they worshiped when Israel got in trouble during the time of Judges. Where were those who would shout, "Glory to Yahweh! Praise Jehovah! Blessed be Jireh!"? Instead, they built altars all over Judah and Jerusalem to worship Baal. Some people never learn their lesson. King Josiah, a godly leader, tried to order the people, in 622 B. C. But, even when Zephaniah came with an urgent message from the Lord, the people were slipping out of the church one by one. Watch out or you will slip away, too!

My second point: It is much closer than what we think. In chapter 1:14-18, they were all crying bitter tears. Even their warrior fled in fear and horror. Yahweh was not playing. His anger came with darkness, blackness, gloom, trouble, and ruin. There was no escape from God's wrath. It was at this point that the Babylonian enemy attacked Judah. They sounded their trumpets and shouted in battle. They charged into each home. Judah was in distress and anguish. Their houses were in ruin. The sky was gray; darkened with the smoke from burning buildings. The towers of the city were defenseless against their attacking enemy. And so, the Babylonians took everyone prisoners into captivity. Nebuchadnezzar conquered. Why do some people have to learn their lessons the hard way?

We have the wonderful Word of God; word by word, step by step instructions on how we are supposed to live peacefully. How much more clearly than this can it be? The word Bible stands for B-basic, I-instructions, B-before, L-leaving, E-earth; basic instructions before leaving earth. And people still try God's patience. They say, "We believe in God." And yet, they still do the things that they can get away with, whether God likes it or not. I am not talking about the sinners. I am talking about those who are saved and still ignore the Ten Commandments of God. We are commanded to edify one another, to lift up one another, but some still tear others down. We are commanded to pray for each other, but still some gossip instead. We are commanded to bear one another's burdens, but some still hide their hand and keep their blessings when they see a brother or a sister in need. One day, our judgment will come, and it will be much sooner than what we think. Maybe, we will get it right before it is too late. Have you confessed the Lord Jesus Christ and truly believe God raised Him from the dead and that Jesus is sitting at the right hand of the Father to make intercession for us?

My third point: It is never too late. The prophet Zephaniah found a few who were sincere and really loved the Lord. He told them to seek three things and the Lord would hide them. They would find God's mercy and escape His wrath and anger. (Zephaniah 2 & 3) He told them to seek the Lord, seek His righteousness, and seek meekness; for they will hide you in the day of God's anger. We need to seek the Lord, seek righteousness, and seek meekness and humility. God will hide us and He will be our shelter from destruction and wrath. "Yahweh" means "He will hide thee." Our enemy is among us, already. There were many who died during the Babylonian War, but few were spared and were exiled to Babylon, because God promised to shelter His people.

It is never too late! Get right with God. Put God first in your life. Zephaniah's warning was not just to Judah and Israel, but to Philistia, Moab, Ammon, Ethiopia, and Assyria. They all suffered through this battle. When Yahweh stretches forth His hand to punish, there is no escape. Remember, God promised to punish disobedience. Are we ready for a new relationship? Seek Jesus and His grace will supply your spirit with salvation. Seek Jesus and He will supply your heart with joy. Seek Jesus and He will supply your feet with strength. Seek Jesus and He will supply your eyes with compassion. Seek Jesus and He will supply you with eternal life. Seek God and His mercy will supply you with everlasting love.

If the Lord should come during the week, are you ready for the judgment day? We all know we are going to be judged, one day, but will it be with rewards in heaven or reproach in hell? God is warning us: "The day of the Lord is at hand." We have all the indications around us. We need to be in church, every Sunday, to hear His message for us. Are we ready, church, for the ending of time? Zephaniah did preach a happy ending to Judah and Israel, and we can have a happy ending, also. But, it has to begin with Jesus. Amen!

About the Author

Paul Gonzalez has a degree in Christian Ministries and is a pastor and certified lay speaker who is dedicated to the art of preaching. He is an avid Bible student and enjoys sharing his knowledge of preaching. Paul lives in Minnesota, plays the harmonica, and is passionate about music and worship.